Kazakhstan Travel Guide 2025-2026

CW01496255

The Essential Kazakhstan Companion: Travel Smart with Local Advice and Itinerary Ideas

Rose Horton

Table of Contents

Introduction 8

Step Into the Heart of Kazakhstan – Where the Unexpected Awaits..... 8

    Why This Guide Is Different 9

    How to Use This Travel Guide 10

Chapter 1 13

Welcome to Kazakhstan ĸz 13

    What Makes It Unique 14

    Quick Facts and Overview... 15

    Why Visit Now? 🧭 🌐 18

    Inspiring Quotes or Traveler Testimonials 19

Chapter 2 21

Travel Planning Essentials.. 21

    Best Time to Visit 21

    Travel Insurance Advice.. 25

    Currency, Exchange Rates, and Budget Planning......................... 27

    Vaccinations & Health Information.. 29

Chapter 3 33

Getting There and Around 🛫 🚗 33

    Major Airports and Entry Points.. 33

Local Transportation Options (Bus, Train, Taxi, Ride-Sharing, Car Rental).. 36

Navigating Public Transport Like a Local 39

Maps, and Directions 40

Eco-Friendly and Budget Transportation Tips............................... 42

Chapter 4 44

Where to Stay 44

Best Neighborhoods to Stay In 44

Accommodation Options (Hotels, Hostels, Resorts, Vacation Rentals) 46

Recommendations for Budget, Mid-range, and Luxury Travelers . 48

Booking Tips and Safety Advice 49

Chapter 5 51

Top Attractions and Experiences... 51

Iconic Landmarks and Must-See Sights............................. 52

Cultural and Historical Highlights 56

Nature and Wildlife Adventures 60

Unique Local Experiences 63

Photography Spots in Kazakhstan.................................... 66

Guided Tours vs. DIY Exploration 69

Chapter 6 72

Off the Beaten Path... 72

Hidden Gems and Local Favorites.. 72

Day Trips and Lesser-Known Towns 74

Scenic Routes and Secret Spots 77

Unusual Attractions Worth Visiting 79

Chapter 7 82

Food and Drink.. 82

Must-Try Local Dishes and Where to Find Them 82

Street Food Scene 85

Best Restaurants and Cafés 88

Local Beverages and Nightlife.. 91

Traditional Beverages 91

Nightlife Hotspots.. 92

Food Etiquette and Tips for Eating Safely.................................... 94

Chapter 8 99

Culture and Traditions 99

History and Heritage... 99

Local Customs and Etiquette 101

Festivals and Celebrations 104

Dress Codes and Social Norms.. 109

Dress Codes for Men and Women 109

Social Etiquette and Manners 111

Language Basics and Key Phrases.. 113

Chapter 9 118

Shopping and Souvenirs 118

    Popular Local Markets and Shopping Streets 118

    Authentic Souvenirs to Bring Home 121

    Haggling Tips 126

    Unique Artisan Products 128

    Where to Buy Unique Artisan Products 132

    Where to Find the Best Deals 133

Chapter 10 141

Adventure and Outdoor Activities 141

    Hiking, Biking, and Outdoor Trails 141

    Water Sports and Beaches 145

    Wildlife Safaris and Nature Parks 149

    Adventure Tours (Zip-lining, Paragliding, etc.) 153

    Safety and Equipment Rental Tips 157

Chapter 11 164

Traveling with Family, Solo, or on a Budget 164

    Family-Friendly Activities and Spots 164

    Tips for Solo Travelers 167

    Budget Itinerary Suggestions 173

    Female Travel Safety Tips 178

    Student and Backpacker Essentials for Traveling in Kazakhstan . 180

Packing Checklist for Backpackers & Students 183

Chapter 12 186

Sustainable and Responsible Travel in Kazakhstan 186

Eco-Friendly Accommodations and Tours 186

Supporting Local Communities 188

Respecting Local Culture and Environment 190

How to Travel Plastic-Free in Kazakhstan 192

Ethical Animal Encounters in Kazakhstan 194

Chapter 13 198

Final Tips and Emergency Information 198

Packing Checklist by Season 198

Local Emergency Numbers and Embassies 200

Foreign Embassies in Kazakhstan 201

Common Scams and How to Avoid Them 203

What to Do in Case of Lost Passport or Illness 205

Departure Tips and Airport Navigation 207

Conclusion 211

Introduction

Step Into the Heart of Kazakhstan – Where the Unexpected Awaits

Welcome to *Kazakhstan Travel Guide 2025–2026*, your ultimate companion to discovering one of Central Asia's most captivating and mysterious destinations. This isn't just a country on the map—it's a living, breathing masterpiece painted in golden steppes, snow-dusted mountains, Soviet legacies, and ancient nomadic traditions. Whether you're an adventure seeker, a culture lover, a digital nomad, or simply someone craving the road less traveled, **Kazakhstan is a place that will redefine how you see the world—and how you see yourself.**

Kazakhstan is the **ninth-largest country in the world**, yet it remains one of the least explored by international travelers. Nestled between Europe and Asia, it offers a rich and intriguing fusion of both continents: **eastern hospitality meets western modernization**, **desert landscapes meet alpine forests**, and **thousand-year-old yurt camps meet futuristic architecture**. This vast country is an open invitation to get lost, to wander, to learn, and to be transformed.

Why This Guide Is Different

This travel guide was not written to simply list landmarks or recycle clichés. It was **crafted with care, cultural insight, and the spirit of discovery** to help you explore Kazakhstan the right way—**authentically, respectfully, and meaningfully.**

- 🔍 **Detailed and Up-to-Date Information (2025–2026)**

  All content is researched with the latest intel so you can plan confidently—be it navigating Astana's dazzling skyline or venturing into the untamed landscapes of Mangystau.

- 🌐 **Cultural Context Beyond the Surface**

  We go beyond "what to do" and dig deep into **why it matters**—from the symbolism behind the dombra's strings to the unwritten rules of dining with nomads.

- 🧳 **For Every Kind of Traveler**

  Whether you're traveling with kids, alone, on a tight budget, or on a luxury escape, this guide has something tailored to you—**it's built to flex and follow your needs.**

- 🖋 **Ethical, Sustainable, and Local-Minded**
  Learn how to travel responsibly, support Kazakh artisans, minimize waste, and honor the land and people whose home you're exploring.

How to Use This Travel Guide

This guide is organized in **clear, easy-to-follow chapters**, each focused on a major aspect of your journey. You can read it cover to cover or jump straight to the topics most relevant to you. Here's a quick breakdown of what you'll find inside:

🏙 CHAPTERS 1–4: Orientation & Planning

These chapters will help you get your bearings: understand Kazakhstan's regions, choose the best time to visit, sort your visa, and plan your routes by train, car, or air, transportation tips, where to stay, and the best of what to see and do.

📍 CHAPTERS 5–6: Top Sights & Hidden Treasures

From iconic landmarks to off-the-grid adventures, you'll get deep dives into where to go and what not to miss—including exact locations, hours, websites 🌐, and travel tips.

🏮 CHAPTER 7: Food & Drink

Prepare your taste buds for fermented mare's milk, sizzling shashlik, and buttery baursak. Find the best local bites and how to enjoy them safely.

🎭 CHAPTERS 8–9: Culture, Shopping & Local Life

Explore Kazakhstan's customs, etiquette, and language essentials. Learn what to buy and where to find the most authentic keepsakes 🛍️.

🧗 CHAPTERS 10–11: Outdoor Thrills & Travel Styles

Plan everything from epic hikes to paragliding, or navigate your trip if you're a family, solo female, student, or budget traveler.

🌿 CHAPTER 12: Sustainable & Responsible Travel

Travel light and travel right—learn how to respect local culture, reduce plastic use, support eco-lodging, and avoid exploitative tourism.

📞 CHAPTER 13: Final Tips & Emergency Info

Before you go, make sure you have **all essential contacts**, emergency numbers 🔢, a **seasonal packing list**, and smart tips for navigating the airport on your way out.

🧭 Quick Navigation Features

To help you move through the guide with ease:

- ⊘ **Clickable Links** for websites, contacts, and resources
- 📍 **Locations** listed with Google Maps-friendly formatting
- 📞 **Contact numbers** for urgent services and bookings
- ✧ **Icons and emojis** to make skimming and referencing more fun

🤍 **A Final Word Before You Begin**

This isn't just a guidebook. It's your gateway to a **nation that welcomes you with a warm "Kosh keldiniz!"** ("Welcome!"). It's a land where **mountains are sacred, stories are passed through song**, and hospitality is a way of life. This journey may begin with curiosity—but if you let it, **it will end with awe.**

So take a deep breath, grab your notebook, charge your camera, and step into the unknown.

Welcome to Kazakhstan.

Your story here is just beginning.

Chapter 1

Welcome to Kazakhstan KZ

Where Nomadic Heritage Meets Futuristic Skylines

Step into the heart of Eurasia, where time-honored nomadic spirit rides alongside space-age ambition. Kazakhstan is a land of endless horizons and ancient stories etched into its mountains, deserts, and steppe. From golden eagles circling the skies to glass towers shimmering under city lights, this vast and varied nation invites you to see, feel, and live something extraordinary — not just a trip, but a journey through cultures, eras, and untamed wonder.

What Makes It Unique

Kazakhstan is a destination like no other — a vast and majestic land where **the ancient rhythms of nomadic life meet 21st-century innovation**. Spanning two continents, **Asia and Europe**, it is the **ninth-largest country in the world**, boasting a staggering diversity of landscapes, cultures, and traditions.

From the shimmering **modern architecture of Nur-Sultan (Astana)** 🏢 to the timeless **steppe plains where wild horses still roam** 🐎, Kazakhstan offers a sensory journey that captures both the future and the past. It's home to **world-class ski resorts**, **otherworldly canyons**, **Soviet ghost towns**, and **Silk Road history**, making it a perfect blend of adventure, heritage, and hospitality.

What truly makes Kazakhstan stand out is its **people** — warm, proud, and fiercely generous. Whether you're sipping **kumis** (fermented mare's milk) in a yurt with locals or trekking the **Tian Shan mountains**, the connections you'll make here are unforgettable.

Unique features include:

- 🌍 **Geographic diversity**: deserts, lakes, mountains, steppe

- ⛰️ **Adventure sports**: skiing, hiking, paragliding, horseback riding

- 🏰 **Cultural richness**: Turkic, Russian, Kazakh, and nomadic traditions

- 🍬 **Space heritage**: Home of the **Baikonur Cosmodrome** 🚀, where the first human went to space

- 🐫 **Nomadic lifestyle**: Still alive through traditions, music, and festivals

Kazakhstan isn't just a destination — it's an **experience** of vastness, resilience, and soul.

Quick Facts and Overview

Get your bearings with this handy overview before diving into Kazakhstan's breathtaking regions.

- **Capital City: Nur-Sultan (Astana)** 🏙️

- **Largest City: Almaty** 🏙️

- **Official Language: Kazakh** (with Russian widely spoken) 🗣️

- **Currency: Kazakhstani Tenge (KZT)** 💰

- **Time Zone**: Varies from **UTC +5 to UTC +6** 🕐

- **Country Code**: +7 ☎

- **Emergency Numbers**:
  - Police: 102
  - Ambulance: 103
  - Fire: 101 🔔

- **Best Time to Visit**:
  - **Spring (April–June)** 🌸 — Blooming landscapes and festivals
  - **Autumn (September–October)** 🍂 — Colorful valleys and ideal weather
  - **Winter (December–February)** ❄ — Perfect for skiing in the mountains
  - **Summer (July–August)** ☀ — Great for hiking, lakes, and outdoor festivals

- **Weather**:
  - Hot, dry summers ☀ (~30–35°C / 86–95°F in July)

- Freezing winters ❄ (~ -20°C / -4°F in January, especially in the north)
- Mountain regions are cooler and ideal for hiking from May to October

- **Religion**: Predominantly **Islam** (Sunni) and **Russian Orthodoxy**

- **Transportation**:
    - Trains 🚇 (affordable and scenic)
    - Domestic flights ✈ (essential for crossing long distances)
    - Marshrutkas (shared minibuses), taxis 🚗, and ride-hailing apps like **Yandex Go**

- **Visa Info**:
    - Many nationalities (including EU, UK, USA) can enter visa-free for up to **30 days**.
    - Check the latest requirements here: 🌐 Kazakhstan Visa Policy

- **Official Tourism Website** 🌐: www.kazakhstan.travel

- **Tourist Info Hotline** ☎: +7 7172 64 72 05

Why Visit Now? 🔍 🌐

There's never been a more exciting time to visit **Kazakhstan** than **2025–2026**. Once a hidden gem for only the most adventurous travelers, the country is now emerging confidently on the global stage with **improved infrastructure, vibrant tourism initiatives**, and **a renewed pride in its cultural heritage**.

Here's why **now is the perfect moment** to experience Kazakhstan:

- **Modern Meets Ancient**: Kazakhstan is rapidly modernizing, with new museums, transport systems, and eco-tourism projects—while fiercely preserving its nomadic roots. You'll witness futuristic cities like **Astana**, where cutting-edge design reflects cosmic ambitions, standing side-by-side with **UNESCO-listed petroglyphs**, ancient caravan routes, and sacred pilgrimage sites.

- **Sustainable Tourism Initiatives** 🌱: The government is investing in **eco-tourism**, supporting **yurt camps, national parks**, and **cultural festivals** that benefit local communities and the environment.

Your trip contributes to meaningful, sustainable growth.

- **Easier Access & Visa-Free Entry** 🛂 : Travelers from over 75 countries now enjoy **visa-free entry**, and with more international flights to Almaty and Astana, it's easier than ever to get here.

- **Global Spotlight Events** 🎉 : Kazakhstan is hosting **regional expos, tech summits, and music festivals**, drawing attention to its dynamic youth, artistic innovation, and global relevance.

- **Off-the-Beaten-Path Adventures** 🏔 : As Europe becomes more crowded with tourists, Kazakhstan remains spacious, untouched, and awe-inspiring. Whether it's hiking the **Charyn Canyon**, stargazing in the **Altai Mountains**, or soaking in the serenity of **Lake Kaindy**, here you can reconnect with nature — and yourself.

Inspiring Quotes or Traveler Testimonials

"**Kazakhstan surprised me in every way — the silence of the steppe, the kindness of strangers, and the colors of Almaty in autumn. It's the kind of place that stays with you long after you've left.**"

— María González, Travel Photographer (Spain)

"If you're searching for authenticity, this is where you'll find it. No filters needed — just raw, real beauty and deep culture."

— Joshua Trent, Travel Blogger (USA)

"One moment I was sipping artisan coffee in a modern cafe, the next I was riding a horse across open grasslands. Kazakhstan is magic — unpredictable, soulful, vast."

— Amina Yusuf, Solo Traveler (Kenya)

"The landscapes reminded me of Mongolia, the cities like Dubai, but the spirit — the spirit is uniquely Kazakh."

— Erik Andersen, Adventure Vlogger (Norway)

Chapter 2

Travel Planning Essentials

Before you set foot in the land of wide skies and wild steppe, there are a few important details to know. This chapter gives you everything you need to plan your Kazakhstan adventure smoothly — from the perfect season to visit to visa rules and border regulations. Smart planning makes for a stress-free journey!

Best Time to Visit

Kazakhstan's vast size means it spans multiple climate zones — from icy winters in the north to sun-drenched deserts in the south. The best time to visit depends on what kind of experience you're seeking.

🌸 Spring (April–June):

One of the most **picturesque and comfortable** times to visit. Fields bloom with wild tulips, temperatures hover between **15°C and 25°C**, and nature is at its greenest. Ideal for **city exploration**, **national parks**, and **road trips** across the steppe.

☼ Summer (July–August):

Expect **hot, dry weather** — up to **35°C in the south**, with cooler temperatures in mountain regions. A great time for **hiking in the Tien Shan Mountains, camping in yurts,** and **exploring Kazakhstan's many lakes and canyons.** Be sure to pack sun protection and water.

🍁 Autumn (September–October):

Autumn offers **clear skies and crisp air**. It's **harvest season**, so markets are full of fresh fruit and festivals abound. Temperatures range from **10°C to 20°C**. Perfect for **photography**, **cultural experiences**, and **mild outdoor adventures**.

❄ Winter (November–March):

Kazakhstan in winter is **harsh but beautiful**. Northern cities like **Astana** often reach **−20°C**, but if you're into **snow sports, frozen lakes**, or **the magic of Kazakh New Year (Nauryz)** celebrations, this is your season. Visit **Shymbulak Ski Resort** 🎿 near Almaty for world-class skiing.

📌 **Pro Tip:** Avoid traveling during **late March to early April** in rural areas, as thawing snow can make roads muddy and impassable.

🎿 **Shymbulak Ski Resort Info:**

🌐 Website: https://shymbulak.com/en

☁ Weather updates: https://meteoblue.com

Visa Requirements and Entry Regulations 🛂📋

Kazakhstan has made **travel more accessible** than ever, with a visa-free policy for many countries and simplified online procedures for others.

⚫ **Visa-Free Entry (as of 2025):**

Citizens of over **75 countries** — including the **USA, UK, Canada, EU nations, UAE, Singapore, South Korea, Japan, and Turkey** — can **enter Kazakhstan without a visa for up to 30 or 90 days**, depending on nationality.

Check full updated list here 👉 Kazakhstan MFA Visa Info 🌐

⚫ E-Visa Available:

If your country isn't on the visa-free list, you can apply for an **e-visa online** via Kazakhstan's official portal. The process is fast (usually within 5 working days) and requires:

- A valid passport (minimum 3 months validity)
- Invitation letter or travel itinerary
- Payment of visa fee via credit/debit card 🖃

🌐 Apply here: https://www.vmp.gov.kz

🛂 Arrival Requirements (2025 Updates):

- **No COVID-19 test required** as of January 2025
- All travelers must **register with local migration police within 3 days**, but this is usually done automatically by hotels or border staff
- **Travel insurance** is not mandatory but **highly recommended** 🛡

📞 For visa support: Kazakhstan Ministry of Foreign Affairs

- ☎Phone: +7 (7172) 720111

- 📧 Email: info@mfa.kz

📌 **Important:** If you plan to travel to **border regions** or **remote nature reserves**, some areas require **special permits**. Ask your tour provider or local authorities.

Travel Insurance Advice

While travel insurance isn't mandatory for entering Kazakhstan, it is **highly recommended**, especially if you plan to explore **remote areas, go hiking, or engage in adventure activities**.

Here's what you should consider when choosing travel insurance for Kazakhstan:

- **Medical Coverage**: Ensure your policy includes **emergency medical expenses, evacuation, and hospitalization**, especially for visits to remote regions like the **Altai Mountains** or **Balkhash Desert**, where medical facilities are limited.

- **Adventure Activities** 🧗: If you're trekking, skiing, horse riding, or participating in extreme sports, confirm these are **explicitly covered** by your insurer. Many standard policies exclude high-risk activities.

- **Trip Cancellation & Delay**: While delays in Kazakhstan are uncommon, **weather** can disrupt plans in winter or spring. Choose a policy that covers **flight cancellations, missed connections**, or **unforeseen trip interruptions**.
- **Lost Luggage & Theft**: While major cities like Almaty and Astana are safe, petty theft can occur in crowded places. Insurance covering **lost or stolen valuables** can be a lifesaver.

📌 **Top Insurance Providers for Kazakhstan (International Travelers)**:

- **World Nomads** 🌐:
  https://www.worldnomads.com
- **SafetyWing** 🌐: https://www.safetywing.com
- **Allianz Travel** 🌐:
  https://www.allianztravelinsurance.com

☎ For emergencies in Kazakhstan:

- Ambulance (Emergency): **103**
- Tourist Helpline (English-speaking): **+7 (7172) 701 323** 📞

Currency, Exchange Rates, and Budget Planning

Kazakhstan uses the **Kazakhstani Tenge (KZT ₸)**, and cash still plays a major role, especially outside of urban areas.

🎴 Currency Overview:

- Coins: **1, 2, 5, 10, 20, 50, 100 tenge**
- Notes: **200, 500, 1,000, 2,000, 5,000, and 20,000 tenge**

☑ Exchange Rate (as of May 2025):

- $1 USD ≈ **455 KZT**
- €1 EUR ≈ **495 KZT**
  (For live updates, check: XE Currency Exchange 🌐)

💳 Card Usage & ATMs:

- Credit and debit cards (Visa/MasterCard) are **widely accepted** in cities, malls, hotels, and restaurants 🏨.

- However, carry cash for **rural areas, markets, taxis**, and **small shops**.
- ATMs are **common in cities** but may not always support foreign cards — look for **Halyk Bank**, **Kaspi**, or **Sberbank** machines.

📍 Recommended Banks for Tourists:

- **Halyk Bank**: https://halykbank.kz ⊕
- **Kaspi Bank**: https://kaspi.kz ⊕

💱 **Where to Exchange Money**:

- Best rates are often found at **official currency exchange offices** in city centers and airports.
- Avoid street changers and always ask for a receipt 🧾.
- Exchange rates at **hotels or airports** are less favorable than city bureaus.

📊 **Daily Budget Estimates (Per Person):**

Budget Type	Daily Cost (KZT)	Daily Cost (USD)
Budget	9,000–15,000 ₸	$20–$35 🪙

Budget Type	Daily Cost (KZT)	Daily Cost (USD)
Mid-range	20,000–40,000 ₸	$45–$90 💼
Luxury	50,000+ ₸	$110+ 🛎

💡 **Budget Tips**:

- Use **Yandex Go app** 🚗 instead of taxis for local transport — it's cheaper and safer.
- Eat like a local! Try **Lagman, Plov, and Beshbarmak** at traditional **canteens (столовая)** for great meals under $5.
- Public transport (metro, buses) in cities is **very cheap**, typically **₸90–150 per ride**.

Vaccinations & Health Information

Ensuring your health and safety while traveling is key to a smooth and enjoyable trip. While Kazakhstan is a relatively **safe destination**, it's still essential to be aware of the health precautions before traveling, especially if you're venturing into remote areas or planning outdoor activities.

💊 **Vaccinations:**

Before heading to Kazakhstan, make sure your routine vaccinations are up-to-date, as well as any recommended travel-specific vaccinations. Here's a breakdown:

- **Routine   Vaccines**:
  Ensure you're up-to-date with general vaccines like **MMR (Measles, Mumps, Rubella)**, **Diphtheria, Tetanus, and Pertussis (DTP)**, **Polio**, and **Flu** (Seasonal) shots.
- **Recommended Vaccines** (For travelers):
  - **Hepatitis A**: Recommended for most travelers due to potential contamination in food or water.
  - **Hepatitis B**: For long-term stays or if you might have medical procedures or unprotected sex.
  - **Typhoid**: Recommended if you plan on visiting rural areas or eating street food.
  - **Rabies**: If you plan to visit remote areas, especially around animals or wildlife (including dogs, bats, and rodents).
  - **Malaria**: Malaria risk is generally **low** in Kazakhstan, but **preventative medication** may be recommended if traveling to rural or border areas, especially in the **south**.

💡 **Visit your healthcare provider** at least **4–6 weeks before departure** to discuss vaccines and obtain any required prescriptions or advice.

🖥️ Health and Safety Tips:

- **Medical Facilities**: **Major cities** like **Almaty** and **Astana** have modern healthcare facilities, including private clinics where English is often spoken. In remote areas, medical infrastructure can be limited, so it's important to have **travel insurance** that covers **emergency evacuation**.

  - **Major Hospital Contacts**:
    - **Almaty International Medical Center**: +7 727 297 63 70
    - **Kazakhstan Clinic (Astana)**: +7 7172 797 222

- **Water & Food Safety**: Tap water in Kazakhstan is **not always potable**. It's best to drink bottled water unless you're certain it's safe. When consuming street food or eating in rural areas, ensure the food is **cooked thoroughly** to avoid **foodborne illnesses**.

  - **Safe Drinking Water Brands**: **Aqua Minerale, Coca-Cola Company Bottled Water** (widely available).

- **Air Quality**: During winter, air quality in cities like **Almaty** and **Astana** can be **poor due to heating and industrial activity**. If you have respiratory issues, it's advisable to carry a **mask** and check air quality updates via apps like **AirVisual** or **IQAir**.

🧴 Travel Health Kit:

Carry a small medical kit with the basics:

- **Prescription Medications**: Ensure you have enough for your entire stay and bring a doctor's note in case customs require it.
- **Over-the-counter Medications**: For common issues like headaches, motion sickness, or digestive troubles.
- **Hand Sanitizer & Wet Wipes**: Handy for keeping clean when water isn't available.
- **Sunscreen & Bug Repellent**: The sun can be harsh, and in some areas, insect bites might be an issue.

📞 Emergency Health Number:

- **Ambulance: 103**
- **Tourist Assistance (English-Speaking): +7 (7172) 701 323**
- **International SOS (Medical Assistance)**: https://www.internationalsos.com

Chapter 3

Getting There and Around 🛫 🚗

Kazakhstan's vast landscapes and bustling cities are well-connected through modern transportation networks, making it easy for travelers to explore every corner of this incredible country. With major international airports in Almaty and Nur-Sultan, along with reliable local transport options like buses, trains, taxis, and ride-sharing services, getting around is a breeze. Whether you're visiting the urban marvels or venturing into the great outdoors, Kazakhstan's transport systems ensure that your journey is smooth and hassle-free. From affordable city buses to scenic train rides across the steppe, every trip offers a unique experience!

Major Airports and Entry Points

Kazakhstan, being the largest country in Central Asia, is well-connected globally and offers several international entry points, especially through major airports in cities like Almaty and Astana (now Nur-Sultan). Here's a breakdown of the key airports:

1. Almaty International Airport (ALA) 🌥

- **Location**: Almaty, the former capital and economic hub of Kazakhstan.
- **Airport Code**: ALA
- **Distance to City Center**: Approximately **15 km** (20 minutes by taxi or shuttle).
- **Key Airlines**: Air Astana, Qatar Airways, Turkish Airlines, Lufthansa, Aeroflot.
- **Facilities**: The airport is modern, with a variety of services like duty-free shopping, restaurants, currency exchange, and free Wi-Fi. It's well-connected to international and regional destinations.
- **Website**: Almaty International Airport 🌐

2. Nursultan Nazarbayev International Airport (TSE) 🌥

- **Location**: Nur-Sultan (formerly Astana), the capital city of Kazakhstan.
- **Airport Code**: TSE
- **Distance to City Center**: Approximately **15 km** (20 minutes by taxi).

- **Key Airlines**: Air Astana, FlyArystan, and international carriers like Emirates, Lufthansa, and Air China.
- **Facilities**: Includes lounges, shops, and restaurants, along with fast immigration services. The airport also has **direct connections to several Central Asian and European cities**.
- **Website**: Nursultan Nazarbayev International Airport 🌐

3. Shymkent International Airport (CIT) 🛩

- **Location**: Shymkent, Kazakhstan's third-largest city in the southern part of the country.
- **Airport Code**: CIT
- **Distance to City Center**: Around **10 km** (15 minutes by taxi).
- **Key Airlines**: Air Astana, FlyArystan.
- **Website**: Shymkent International Airport 🌐

4. Aktau International Airport (SCO) 🛬

- **Location**: Aktau, located on the western coast of Kazakhstan, along the Caspian Sea.
- **Airport Code**: SCO

- **Distance to City Center**: Approximately **25 km** (30 minutes by taxi).
- **Key Airlines**: Air Astana, SCAT Airlines.
- **Website**: <u>Aktau International Airport</u> 🌐

Entry Regulations 🛂:

- **Visa Requirements**: Most travelers need a **visa** to enter Kazakhstan, unless they come from one of the visa-exempt countries (e.g., Russia, Ukraine, and several other CIS countries). For detailed visa requirements, check with the <u>Kazakh Embassy</u>.
- **Customs**: Kazakhstan has strict customs rules. Ensure you declare any high-value items like electronics or large amounts of cash (over $10,000). Personal items for personal use are generally allowed.

Local Transportation Options (Bus, Train, Taxi, Ride-Sharing, Car Rental)

Once you've arrived in Kazakhstan, getting around is straightforward thanks to a variety of local transport options. Here's a guide to help you navigate the cities and beyond:

🚌 Buses:

- **Public Buses** are an affordable way to get around major cities like Almaty, Nur-Sultan, and Shymkent. Tickets cost around **₸90–150** and are available directly from the driver.
- **Night Buses**: Some cities also operate **night buses** that run on specific routes, making it easy to get around after hours.

🚆 Trains:

- **Train Travel** is an essential part of Kazakhstan's transportation network, especially for long-distance travel between major cities like Almaty, Nur-Sultan, and Atyrau.
- The trains are comfortable, with several classes available, including **luxury sleeper cabins** for overnight travel.
- **Booking**: You can purchase tickets online via the **Kazakhstan Railways website** KTZ.

🚕 Taxis:

- **Taxis** are widely available in cities. You can hail a taxi on the street, or use taxi apps like **Yandex.Taxi** or **Uber** for more convenience.
- Fares within cities range from **₸500 to ₸2,000**, depending on the distance.
- **Tip**: Agree on the fare before starting the journey to avoid surprises.

🚗 Ride-Sharing (Yandex.Go & Uber):

- **Yandex.Go** is the leading ride-sharing service in Kazakhstan, much like Uber, and operates in **major cities**. You can book a ride via the app, which will give you the estimated fare before confirming the ride.
- **Uber** is also available in cities like Almaty and Nur-Sultan, offering an efficient and safe travel experience.

🚐 Car Rental:

- If you're planning to explore rural areas, national parks, or need more flexibility, **renting a car** is a great option.

- Rental companies like **Avis**, **Europcar**, and **Hertz** operate in major cities and at airports. The daily rental cost starts from ₸**8,000** ($18) for compact cars, with additional costs for insurance, fuel, and other add-ons.
- **Driving License**: International travelers may need an **International Driving Permit (IDP)** along with their home-country driving license.

🚲 **Bicycles:**

- For short distances, **cycling** is becoming increasingly popular, especially in **Almaty**, where there are **dedicated bike lanes**.
- Bike rental shops offer daily rentals for approximately ₸**2,000**–₸**5,000**.

Navigating Public Transport Like a Local

Kazakhstan's public transport system offers a blend of convenience and efficiency, especially in major cities like **Almaty** and **Nur-Sultan**. To get around like a local, here are some tips:

- **Bus Travel**: Public buses are affordable and widely used. Locals typically use a **single-use card** or **QR codes** to pay for their fares, which are available at kiosks and onboard. Don't forget to look for the bus number that matches your route!
- **Metro (Nur-Sultan)**: The metro in **Nur-Sultan** (previously Astana) is efficient and easy to navigate. It's the fastest way to cover long distances within the city. Tickets are purchased at kiosks or through mobile apps.
- **Trams**: In **Almaty**, you'll find trams that are an iconic way to travel through the city. Although not as extensive as buses, they cover key areas and are particularly useful for scenic city routes.

Pro Tip: If you're not familiar with the routes, don't hesitate to ask locals for help. They are generally friendly and happy to guide you.

Maps, and Directions

Knowing where you're headed is key to a smooth journey in Kazakhstan. Here's how to stay on track:

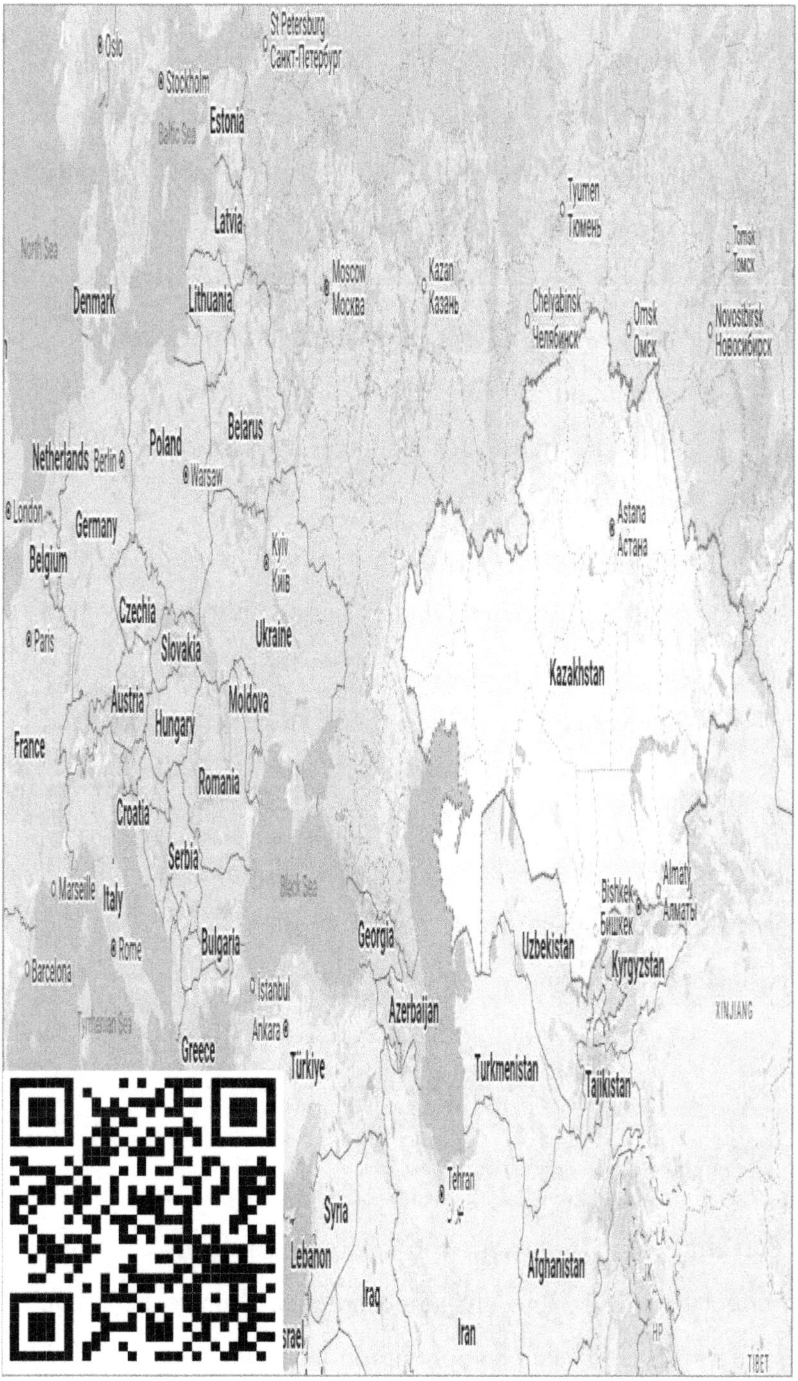
St Petersburg
Санкт-Петербург
Oslo
Stockholm
Baltic Sea
Estonia
Latvia
North Sea
Tyumen
Тюмень
Tomsk
Томск
Moscow
Москва
Kazan
Казань
Denmark
Lithuania
Chelyabinsk
Челябинск
Omsk
Омск
Novosibirsk
Новосибирск
Belarus
Poland
Netherlands
Berlin
Warsaw
London
Germany
Astana
Астана
Belgium
Kyiv
Київ
Czechia
Ukraine
Paris
Slovakia
Kazakhstan
Austria
Moldova
Hungary
France
Romania
Croatia
Serbia
Black Sea
Marseille
Italy
Bishkek
Бишкек
Almaty
Алматы
Rome
Bulgaria
Georgia
Uzbekistan
Kyrgyzstan
Barcelona
Istanbul
Azerbaijan
XINJIANG
Tyrrhenian Sea
Ankara
Greece
Türkiye
Turkmenistan
Tajikistan
Tehran
Syria
Lebanon
Afghanistan
Iraq
Iran
srael
LA
JK
HP
TIBET

- **Google Maps**: Google Maps is widely used in Kazakhstan, with accurate directions for public transport, walking, and driving. It's highly recommended for navigating the cities and beyond.
- **Yandex Maps**: Another popular choice is **Yandex Maps**, which also provides detailed public transport routes and traffic information in real time. It's especially handy for ride-sharing services and taxi bookings.
- **Offline Maps**: If you're heading to more remote areas or worried about connectivity, download offline maps from apps like **Maps.me** or **CityMaps2Go**, which offer detailed maps and walking directions without needing internet access.

Tip: Street signs in Kazakhstan are often bilingual, but it's always useful to have the names written in **Cyrillic** for easier understanding.

Eco-Friendly and Budget Transportation Tips

Traveling in Kazakhstan can be both eco-conscious and budget-friendly! Here are some practical tips to help you save money and reduce your carbon footprint:

- **Public Transport**: The most eco-friendly way to get around is using public transport. Buses, trams, and the metro in **Nur-Sultan** are not only affordable but also an easy way to reduce your environmental impact. A single bus ride costs as little as ₸90, and metro tickets are also budget-friendly.
- **Ride-Sharing Services**: Apps like **Yandex.Go** and **Uber** are great for carpooling, allowing you to share rides with others, which can help lower your transportation costs while minimizing emissions.
- **Cycling**: In cities like **Almaty**, biking is not only a healthy and green way to travel, but it's also a **budget-friendly option**. Many rental shops offer bikes for as low as **₸2,000 per day**.
- **Walkable Cities**: Kazakhstan's cities, particularly **Almaty**, are quite **walkable**, especially in the city center. Walking saves money on transport and gives you the chance to explore the local culture up close.

Pro Tip: For longer trips between cities, **trains** are an eco-friendly alternative to flying and provide comfortable travel with scenic views.

Chapter 4

Where to Stay

Kazakhstan offers a wide range of accommodations to suit every type of traveler, whether you're looking for luxury, comfort, or a budget-friendly stay. From bustling cities to tranquil retreats, the country's diverse neighborhoods and lodging options make it easy to find a place that fits your needs. Whether you're exploring the cosmopolitan vibe of **Almaty**, the futuristic architecture of **Nur-Sultan**, or the charming beauty of **Shymkent**, you'll find welcoming options that allow you to rest and recharge after a day of adventure.

Best Neighborhoods to Stay In

When visiting Kazakhstan, choosing the right neighborhood can enhance your experience. Here are some of the best areas to stay in the major cities:

- **Almaty**:
  - **City Center**: The heart of Almaty, where you'll find a mix of cultural attractions, shopping, and dining. It's close to landmarks

like **Zenkov Cathedral** and **Medeu Ice Rink**.

- o **Panfilov Park Area**: Ideal for nature lovers, this area offers peaceful parks and access to the nearby mountains.
- o **Bostandyk**: A trendy district with cafes, shopping malls, and easy access to public transport.

- **Nur-Sultan (Astana)**:
  - o **Downtown Nur-Sultan**: This is the most futuristic part of the city, with iconic architecture like the **Bayterek Tower** and **Khan Shatyr** shopping center. It's perfect for those wanting to be in the midst of the city's modern hustle and bustle.
  - o **Left Bank**: Known for government buildings and the **Palace of Peace and Reconciliation**, this area offers quieter, upscale accommodations.

- **Shymkent**:
  - o **Central Shymkent**: With easy access to the city's historical sites and local markets, this area is perfect for first-time visitors.

o **Aksu**: A bit further out but offers a more relaxed atmosphere with local parks and traditional markets.

Accommodation Options (Hotels, Hostels, Resorts, Vacation Rentals)

Kazakhstan offers a wide variety of accommodation types, catering to all budgets and preferences. Here's what to expect:

- **Luxury Hotels**:
  - **Ritz-Carlton** (Almaty & Nur-Sultan): Known for its opulence and top-tier service. The **Ritz-Carlton** in Almaty offers panoramic views of the surrounding mountains.
  - **InterContinental Hotel** (Almaty): A sleek hotel offering modern amenities and views of the city skyline.
- **Mid-Range Hotels**:
  - **Holiday Inn** (Almaty & Nur-Sultan): A reliable international chain providing great amenities, ideal for business travelers.

- **Hotel Kazakhstan** (Almaty): Located in a prime area, this hotel combines comfort and accessibility.
- **Budget-Friendly Hostels**:
  - **Green Hostel** (Almaty): A vibrant place for young travelers, with a friendly atmosphere and easy access to the city's attractions.
  - **Shymkent Hostel** (Shymkent): A great option for budget travelers, offering basic but clean accommodations near local markets.
- **Resorts**:
  - **Shymbulak Ski Resort** (Almaty): For those looking to hit the slopes in winter, **Shymbulak** offers resorts with ski-in, ski-out accommodations.
  - **Burabay Resort** (near Nur-Sultan): Located near the **Burabay National Park**, this resort offers a perfect getaway with stunning lakeside views and nature activities.
- **Vacation Rentals**:
  - **Airbnb** is popular in Kazakhstan, especially for travelers looking for homier and more private stays. You'll find a wide range of

options from city apartments to cozy houses in quiet neighborhoods.

- ○ **Booking.com** also offers vacation rentals, including charming apartments and houses in places like **Almaty** and **Nur-Sultan**.

Pro Tip: During peak tourist seasons, it's a good idea to book accommodations in advance, especially in popular cities like **Almaty** and **Nur-Sultan**, to secure the best rates and availability.

Recommendations for Budget, Mid-range, and Luxury Travelers

Kazakhstan offers something for every traveler, whether you're looking to save, indulge, or find a balance between comfort and affordability:

- **Budget Travelers**: Hostels like **Green Hostel** in **Almaty** or **Shymkent Hostel** offer basic but clean accommodations at affordable rates. For more privacy, Airbnb offers great options for budget-conscious travelers.

- **Mid-range Travelers**: Hotels like **Holiday Inn** in both **Almaty** and **Nur-Sultan** provide a great mix of comfort, modern amenities, and competitive prices. **Hotel Kazakhstan** in Almaty is another solid option for a comfortable stay without breaking the bank.

- **Luxury Travelers**: For those seeking top-tier experiences, indulge in the luxury of the **Ritz-Carlton** or **InterContinental** in **Almaty**. For a lakeside escape, **Burabay Resort** offers stunning views and five-star services.

Booking Tips and Safety Advice

Booking your stay in Kazakhstan can be made easy with a few simple tips:

- **Book Early**: Particularly during peak seasons (summer and winter holidays), it's best to book your accommodations in advance to secure the best deals and availability.

- **Use Trusted Platforms**: Stick to well-known booking websites like **Booking.com**, **Airbnb**, and

Hotels.com for reliable customer service and secure payment options.

- **Check Reviews**: Before confirming your booking, read reviews from previous guests to ensure the accommodation meets your expectations.

- **Safety Tips**: Kazakhstan is generally safe for travelers, but always take precautions such as locking doors, using hotel safes for valuables, and avoiding isolated areas at night. If you're traveling in more remote areas, it's always a good idea to let someone know your whereabouts.

Chapter 5

Top Attractions and Experiences

Discover Kazakhstan's Wonders — From Timeless Monuments to Modern Marvels

Kazakhstan is a country where natural grandeur and cultural depth collide in spectacular fashion. Whether you're chasing legends on the vast steppe, marveling at Soviet-era engineering, or soaking up panoramic views from futuristic towers, this land offers **endless surprises**. The diversity of attractions — from ancient burial mounds and UNESCO World Heritage Sites to shimmering skyscrapers and silk road bazaars — means there's something to awe and inspire every kind of traveler.

This chapter guides you through the **most iconic landmarks, unforgettable experiences, and cultural jewels** of Kazakhstan, helping you plan your itinerary around **the best of the best**.

Iconic Landmarks and Must-See Sights

1. Bayterek Tower – Nur-Sultan (Astana) 🏛️ ◯

A symbol of Kazakhstan's bold future and folklore-rich past, Bayterek Tower stands tall at 105 meters in the capital city. Its golden sphere represents the mythical "Tree of Life" and the sacred egg of the Samruk bird from Kazakh legend.

- 📍 **Location**: Nur-Sultan city center, near Nurzhol Boulevard
- 🕐 **Opening Hours**: 10:00 AM – 8:00 PM (Closed Mondays)
- 💰 **Entry Fee**: 1000 KZT (~$2.20)
- 🌐 Visit Website
- 📞 **Contact**: +7 7172 57 89 00 ☎️

Ride the elevator to the top for panoramic views of the city — especially magical at sunset!

2. Charyn Canyon – Almaty Region 🗺️ 📷

Known as Kazakhstan's "Grand Canyon," Charyn is a geological wonder shaped over 12 million years. The **Valley of Castles** area is a must-see for its dramatic red rock formations and alien-like terrain.

- 📍 **Location**: ~200 km east of Almaty (4-hour drive)
- 🕐 **Open Year-Round**
- 💰 **Entry Fee**: 750 KZT (~$1.65)
- 🌐 Visit Website
- 📞 **Contact (Almaty Parks Office)**: +7 727 275 43 60 ☎️

You can camp, hike, or join guided day trips from Almaty. Don't forget your camera — this place is stunning.

3. Mausoleum of Khoja Ahmed Yasawi – Turkistan 🏛️🕊️

A masterpiece of **Timurid architecture**, this UNESCO World Heritage Site is a spiritual beacon and one of Kazakhstan's holiest landmarks. Built in the 14th century, it's a place of pilgrimage and a window into medieval craftsmanship.

- 📍 **Location**: Turkistan, South Kazakhstan
- 🕐 **Opening Hours**: 9:00 AM – 7:00 PM daily
- 💰 **Entry Fee**: Free (small museum fee inside)
- 🌐 Visit Website
- 📞 **Contact**: +7 7253 30 26 77 ☎️

Don't miss the giant copper cauldron used for rituals and the intricately tiled domes.

4. Baikonur Cosmodrome – Baikonur 🚀 🌑

The **world's first and largest spaceport**, Baikonur is where Sputnik launched and Yuri Gagarin made history. A guided visit here is like walking through the pages of space history.

- 📍 **Location**: Baikonur City, Kyzylorda Region
- 🕐 **Tours**: Must be booked in advance (passport required)
- 💰 **Packages**: Vary by agency (~$800–$1500 for full experience)
- 🌐 Visit Baikonur Space Tours
- 📞 **Tour Inquiries**: +7 701 728 88 88 ☎

Bonus: Time your visit to witness a **live rocket launch**.

5. Big Almaty Lake – Almaty Region 🏔 💧

Cradled in the **Ile-Alatau National Park**, this turquoise alpine lake sits at over 2500 meters above sea level and is a postcard-perfect escape from the city.

- 📍 **Location**: ~28 km south of Almaty
- 🕐 **Best Visit Time**: May to October
- 💰 **Entry Fee**: 500 KZT (~$1.10) + Transport
- 🌐 Visit Website
- 📞 **Park Info**: +7 727 233 14 04 ☎

No swimming allowed (it's a drinking water source), but photography and picnics are highly encouraged.

Cultural and Historical Highlights

1. National Museum of the Republic of Kazakhstan – Nur-Sultan 🏛️🏢

A must-visit for understanding Kazakhstan's **ancient roots to modern nationhood**, this museum showcases everything from Bronze Age artifacts to contemporary art.

- 📍 **Location**: 54 Tauelsizdik Avenue, Nur-Sultan
- 🕐 **Opening Hours**: 10:00 AM – 6:00 PM (Closed Mondays)
- 💰 **Entry Fee**: 1000 KZT (~$2.20)
- 🌐 Official Site
- 📞 **Contact**: +7 7172 91 90 35 ☎

The highlight? The **Golden Man** – a fully adorned warrior from the 4th century BC.

2. Ethno-Memorial Complex "Map of Kazakhstan – Atameken" – Nur-Sultan 🗺️🏠

This outdoor cultural park is a miniature **3D map** of Kazakhstan where visitors can walk through the entire country in an hour — complete with models of its major landmarks.

- 📍 **Location**: 2 Turan Avenue, Nur-Sultan
- 🕐 **Opening Hours**: 10:00 AM – 7:00 PM

- 💰 **Entry Fee**: 600 KZT (~$1.30)
- 🌐 Visit Website
- 📞 **Contact**: +7 7172 24 02 94 ☎

Perfect for families or those short on travel time.

3. Korkyt Ata Memorial Complex – Kyzylorda Region 🎵📷

Dedicated to the legendary philosopher-musician Korkyt Ata, this site combines **ancient Turkic heritage, myth, and sound art**. The wind-powered musical sculptures here literally play with the steppe breeze.

- 📍 **Location**: 18 km from Zhosaly, Kyzylorda Region
- 🕐 **Open Year-Round**
- 💰 **Entry Fee**: Free
- 📞 **Cultural Office Contact**: +7 7242 27 44 70 ☎

The fusion of wind, tradition, and technology makes this a spiritual and sensory journey.

4. Aisha Bibi Mausoleum – Taraz 🗺️🏠

A romantic and architectural treasure, this 11th-century mausoleum is famous for its ornate terracotta patterns and the tragic love story behind it.

- 📍 **Location**: 18 km from Taraz, Zhambyl Region
- 🕐 **Opening Hours**: 9:00 AM – 6:00 PM
- 💰 **Entry Fee**: Free
- 📞 **Tour Info**: +7 7262 51 45 90 ☎️

Often visited by couples and wedding parties seeking blessings for love and loyalty.

5. Abai House-Museum – Semey 📖✏️

Explore the life and legacy of **Abai Kunanbayev**, Kazakhstan's national poet and philosopher. His home-turned-museum offers rare manuscripts, musical instruments, and personal belongings.

- 📍 **Location**: 5 Abai Street, Semey
- 🕐 **Opening Hours**: 10:00 AM – 5:00 PM (Closed Sundays)
- 💰 **Entry Fee**: 500 KZT (~$1.10)

- 📞 **Contact**: +7 7222 56 78 22 ☎️

A pilgrimage site for lovers of literature and Kazakh identity.

Nature and Wildlife Adventures

Kazakhstan's wild heart beats strongest in its national parks, alpine lakes, and desert oases. Embark on journeys that bring you face-to-face with eagles, horses, and ancient ecosystems.

1. Altyn Emel National Park – "Singing Dunes" & Wildlife 🏜️🐫

Feel the Sahara of Central Asia come alive at the 150-meter-high **Singing Dune**, whose sand "sings" when the wind blows. Beyond the desert, the park shelters **Przewalski's horses**, **Bactrian camels**, and over 300 bird species.

- 📍 **Location**: 300 km northeast of Almaty (near Kapshagay Reservoir)
- 🕐 **Best Season**: May–September (warm days, cool nights)

- 💰 **Entry Fee**: 1 200 KZT (~$2.60)

- 🌐 Website: kazakhstan.travel/nature/altyn-emel

- ☎ Contact: +7 727 270 30 40

- 📍 Address: Altyn Emel Entrance Gate, Almaty Region 📍

2. Kolsai & Kaindy Lakes – Alpine Serenity 🏔️✂️

Tucked into the northern Tian Shan, the three **emerald-green Kolsai Lakes** and the underwater forest of **Kaindy Lake** offer scenic hiking (12 km round-trip) and horseback rides along crystal waters.

- 📍 **Location**: 330 km southeast of Almaty

- 🕐 **Best Season**: June–October (gentle temperatures)

- 💰 **Entry Fee**: 800 KZT (~$1.75)

- 🌐 Website: kazakhstan.travel/nature/kolsai-lakes

- ☎ Contact: +7 727 233 14 04

- 📍 Address: Kolsai Lakes Visitor Center, Ile-Alatau NP 📍

3. Burabay National Park – Forests & Granite Mountains 🌳⛰️

Also known as **"Kazakh Switzerland,"** Burabay is a forested lake district with sculpted granite peaks like **Okzhetpes** and **Map Hill**. Boat cruises, cycling trails, and spa resorts make this a year-round retreat.

- 📍 **Location**: 250 km north of Nur-Sultan
- 🕐 **Open**: Year-round (ice fishing & skiing in winter)
- 💰 **Entry Fee**: 600 KZT (~$1.30)
- 🌐 Website: kazakhstan.travel/nature/burabay 🌐
- ☎️ Contact: +7 71636 4 73 15
- 📍 Address: Burabay Park HQ, Akmola Region 📍

4. Saryarka Steppe – Birdwatcher's Paradise 🦩🕊️

A UNESCO-listed biosphere reserve, **Saryarka** is famed for **flamingos**, **pelicans**, and **white pelicans**, alongside vast grasslands that echo with the calls of migrating cranes. Ideal for spring and autumn bird migrations.

- 📍 **Location**: 40 km north of Nur-Sultan

- 🕐 **Best Season**: April–May & September–October
- 💰 **Entry Fee**: Free (guided tours extra)
- 🌐 Website: kazakhstan.travel/nature/saryarka 🌐
- ☎ Contact: +7 7172 25 13 46
- 📍 Address: Saryarka Visitor Center, Akmola Region 📍

Unique Local Experiences

Dive into Kazakhstan's living traditions — from nomadic hospitality to culinary workshops and festivals that bring ancient customs into the modern era.

1. Nomadic Yurt Stay & Kumis Tasting 🏔🥛

Spend a night in a **traditional Kazakh yurt**, learning to erect the felt-covered dwelling and share kumis (fermented mare's milk) with your host family. Live music from the **dombra** and star-filled skies complete the experience.

- 📍 **Locations**: Altyn-Emel, Kolsai Lakes, Charyn Canyon camps
- 🌐 Book via: kazakhstan.travel/experiences/yurt-stay

- ☎ Contact: +7 727 270 30 40

2. Eagle Hunting Demonstrations – Almaty & East Kazakhstan 🦅❄

Meet **kazakh berkutchi** (eagle hunters) and watch them command golden eagles to swoop and catch prey. Often paired with falconry workshops where you handle the majestic birds yourself.

- 📍 **Locations**: Almaty foothills & Karaganda region
- 🕐 **Season**: October–March (eagles in hunting season)
- 🌐 Website: kazakhstan.travel/culture/eagle-hunting 🌐
- ☎ Contact: +7 701 234 56 78

3. Green Bazaar Culinary Tour – Almaty 🥕🛍

Wander through the bustling **Almaty Green Bazaar**, sampling **baursaks**, **qazy** (horse sausage), fresh berries, and spices. Learn to haggle like a local and take home recipe tips from market vendors.

- 📍 **Location**: 45a Zenkov Street, Almaty

- ⏱ **Hours**: 7:00 AM–6:00 PM daily
- 🌐 Website: none (meet guide at entrance)
- ☎ Contact: +7 727 263 49 21

4. Nauryz Festival – Spring Renewal 🎽🎷

Celebrate the **Persian New Year** (March 21–23) with open-air concerts, horse games (kokpar), and communal feasts of **Nauryz kozhe** (seven-ingredient soup). Cities and villages across Kazakhstan host their own unique festivities.

- 📍 **Major Celebrations**: Nur-Sultan, Almaty, Turkistan
- ⏱ **Dates**: March 21–23 annually
- 🌐 Website: kazakhstan.travel/events/nauryz 🌐
- ☎ Contact: +7 7172 64 72 05

5. Beshbarmak Cooking Masterclass – Nationwide 🍽👨‍🍳

Learn to prepare **beshbarmak**, Kazakhstan's national dish of boiled meat and hand-cut noodles. Classes include dough rolling, broth simmering, and serving traditions.

- 📍 **Locations**: Almaty, Nur-Sultan, Karaganda
- 🌐 Book via:

  kazakhstan.travel/experiences/beshbarmak
- ☎ Contact: +7 7172 91 90 35

Photography Spots in Kazakhstan

Kazakhstan is a dream canvas for photographers — a place where vast steppes, glacial lakes, futuristic skylines, and ancient ruins blend into a single dramatic shot. Whether you're a professional or just traveling with a smartphone, you'll find unforgettable frames across the country.

1. Charyn Canyon – The Grand Canyon's Cousin 🏞

Famed for its **Valley of Castles**, Charyn's rusty-orange cliffs glow during sunrise and sunset, offering captivating silhouettes and light contrasts. Drone-friendly zones make it ideal for aerial shots.

- 📍 **Location**: 200 km east of Almaty
- 🕐 **Best Light**: Sunrise (6–7 AM) and Golden Hour (5–6 PM)
- 🌐 Info: kazakhstan.travel/nature/charyn-canyon
- ☎ Contact: +7 727 273 00 55

2. Kaindy Lake – The Submerged Forest

This surreal lake has **sunken spruce trees** standing tall in turquoise water, creating haunting reflections and ethereal beauty. Ideal for long-exposure and reflection shots.

- 📍 **Location**: Near Saty Village, 300 km from Almaty
- 🕐 **Best Season**: Autumn for colorful foliage
- 🌐 Info: kazakhstan.travel/nature/kaindy-lake 🌐

3. Bayterek Tower – Icon of Nur-Sultan 🏢

The futuristic capital's most iconic structure offers a great subject during twilight. Capture the tower against the vivid sky or take panoramic cityscapes from the observation deck.

- 📍 **Location**: Nur-Sultan City Center
- 🕐 **Best Shot**: Blue hour (just after sunset)
- 🌐 Info: bayterek.kz

4. Bozzhyra Canyon – Alien Landscape 🏔️

Located on the **Mangystau Plateau**, this little-known spot stuns with lunar rock formations and isolated cliffs — one of the most photogenic desert scenes in Central Asia.

- 📍 **Location**: Mangystau Region, near Zhanaozen
- 🕐 **Lighting Tip**: Capture shadows across ridges at dawn
- 🌐 Info: kazakhstan.travel/nature/bozzhyra

5. Turkistan – Architectural Heritage 🏛️

The **Mausoleum of Khoja Ahmed Yasawi** glows beautifully under night lights. Inside, you'll find symmetric tile patterns and spiritual tranquility for architectural and cultural photography.

- 📍 **Location**: Turkistan City
- 🕐 **Best Light**: Evening blue hour + interior daylight shots
- 🌐 Info: kazakhstan.travel/culture/turkistan

Guided Tours vs. DIY Exploration

When traveling Kazakhstan, you'll need to decide between **guided tours** and **do-it-yourself (DIY)** exploration. Both offer distinct benefits, depending on your travel style, language skills, and desired depth of experience.

🎧 Guided Tours

Perfect for: First-time travelers, cultural immersion seekers, non-Russian/Kazakh speakers

Advantages:

- ☑ Hassle-free transportation and logistics
- ☑ Local guides offer **rich history, legends, and insider access**
- ☑ Often includes meals, entrance fees, and permits

- ☑ Great for **remote areas** like **Altyn Emel**, **Bozzhyra**, or **Baikonur Cosmodrome**

Top Guided Tour Providers in Kazakhstan:

- **Nomadic Travel Kazakhstan** – nomadic.kz 🌐 / +7 701 000 1111 ☎
- **KAZ Treks** – kaztreks.com 🌐 / +7 702 333 2233 ☎
- **Steppe Spirit** – steppespirit.kz 🌐 / +7 747 888 9494 ☎

📖 **DIY Travel**

Perfect for: Independent adventurers, repeat visitors, budget travelers

Advantages:

- ☑ Freedom to explore at your own pace
- ☑ Budget-friendly, especially with shared taxis and trains
- ☑ Chance to **meet locals organically**

- ☑️ Great for **city tours**, **markets**, and **main attractions** (e.g., Bayterek, Medeu, Kok Tobe)

Tips for DIY Success:

- 📱 **Download offline maps** (Maps.me, Yandex Maps)
- 🈯 Learn basic Russian/Kazakh phrases or carry a translation app
- 🚕 Use **Yandex Go** or **inDrive** for local taxis
- 🏨 Book lodging near landmarks to save time and cost

Verdict?

- For **rugged nature** and **language-barrier zones**, go **guided**.
- For **urban cities**, **photography**, and **slow travel**, go **DIY**.

Chapter 6

Off the Beaten Path

Kazakhstan's raw, wide-open beauty hides more than the well-known peaks of Almaty or the shining towers of Nur-Sultan. Away from the usual trails lie untouched treasures — sleepy towns, sacred sites, dramatic valleys, and intimate cultural experiences. This chapter will guide you through these **hidden gems and lesser-known escapes** that reveal the soul of Kazakhstan beyond the spotlight.

Hidden Gems and Local Favorites

🏠 Tamgaly Petroglyphs – Ancient Rock Art Gallery

A UNESCO World Heritage Site, Tamgaly's cliffs are etched with **over 5,000 petroglyphs** — animals, rituals, and sun-headed deities dating back to the Bronze Age. Surrounded by steppe silence, it feels like stepping into ancient whispers of humanity.

- 📍 *Location*: 170 km northwest of Almaty
- 🚗 *How to Get There*: Private taxi or group tour
- 🌐 Website: whc.unesco.org/en/list/1145

- ☎ Contact: +7 727 267 60 30

🏠 Aisha Bibi Mausoleum – Love Story in Stone

This elegant 11th-century tomb tells a local tale of forbidden love. Its **carved terracotta tiles** and spiritual calm make it a cherished place for locals and a serene photo spot for travelers.

- 📍 *Location*: Jambyl Region, near Taraz
- 🌐 Website: kazakhstan.travel/culture/aisha-bibi

🏠 Kolsai Lakes – The Blue Necklace of the Tien Shan

While Kaindy Lake gets the fame, the **Kolsai trio of lakes** nearby is a peaceful escape into pine forests, mirror-like waters, and alpine air. Great for hiking, horseback riding, and stargazing.

- 📍 *Location*: Almaty Region, near Saty Village
- ⛰ *Stay*: Guesthouses or eco-yurts in Saty
- 🌐 Website: kazakhstan.travel/nature/kolsai-lakes

🏔 Sherkala Mountain – The Sleeping Lion

In Mangystau's surreal desert, Sherkala rises like a fortress or lion at rest. Locals believe it's a sacred mountain. Few tourists reach here, making it perfect for meditation, exploration, and storytelling.

- 📍 *Location*: Mangystau Region
- 📷 *Tip*: Visit at sunset for golden photos

🐪 Ethno Villages and Nomadic Camps

Want to sleep in a yurt, ride a horse across open plains, or learn to cook **beshbarmak**? Local-run ethno villages near Almaty and Turkistan offer immersive nomadic experiences with fewer tourists.

- 🌐 Explore: nomadethno.kz | ethno-village.kz

Day Trips and Lesser-Known Towns

🏛 Taraz – Silk Road Survivor

One of Kazakhstan's oldest cities, Taraz was a Silk Road hub. Today, it offers well-preserved mausoleums, quiet tea houses, and **a strong Sufi heritage** — without the crowds.

- 🕰 *Highlights*: Tekturmas Complex, Karakhan Mausoleum
- 🚌 *How to Get There*: Daily buses or flights from Almaty and Nur-Sultan
- 🌐 Website: kazakhstan.travel/culture/taraz

🧴 Aral – The Ghosts of the Sea

Once a thriving fishing port on the Aral Sea, Aral is now a haunting reminder of environmental disaster — complete with **ship graveyards** and a growing ecotourism movement. A moving, educational detour.

- 📍 *Location*: Kyzylorda Region
- 🏛 *Must-Visit*: Aral Sea Museum
- 🌐 Learn More: aral2025.org

🍃 Zharkent – A Crossroads of Culture

A small border town known for its incredible **Chinese-style mosque**, Zharkent is a melting pot of Central Asian, Russian, and Dungan (Chinese Muslim) cultures.

- 📍 *Location*: Eastern Kazakhstan

- 🏛️ *Don't Miss*: Zharkent Mosque (built without a single nail!)
- 🌐 Details: kazakhstan.travel/culture/zharkent

🏛️ Sauran – Kazakhstan's Forgotten Fortress

North of Turkistan, Sauran's **crumbling ancient walls** and city ruins sprawl across the steppe — a reminder of the mighty Kazakh Khanates. Walk through silence and history.

- 📍 *Location*: 40 km from Turkistan
- ⏰ *Ideal Time*: Sunrise or late afternoon
- 🌐 Info: kazakhstan.travel/history/sauran

🐪 Baikonur Town – Gateway to the Stars

Often overlooked, Baikonur is home to the **world's oldest spaceport** still in operation. Visit this space town to feel the weight of cosmic history — and maybe catch a rocket launch.

- 📍 *Location*: Kyzylorda Region (permit required)
- 🕐 *Tip*: Book with a licensed space tour operator
- 🌐 Info: roscosmos.ru

🛩 Pro Tip:

For the best off-the-beaten-path experience, **connect with locals**, use **community-led tour platforms**, and **learn a few Kazakh or Russian phrases** to unlock doors to warm hospitality.

Scenic Routes and Secret Spots

Kazakhstan's vastness is best experienced on the road — where miles of golden steppe, jagged cliffs, and whispering deserts reveal their secrets to those willing to explore beyond the usual routes. Below are scenic drives and nature escapes that bring the country's raw beauty into full view.

🏔 Almaty to Charyn Canyon via the Kegen Route

Forget the direct highway — take the longer Kegen route through Saty Village to Charyn Canyon. This winding mountain road passes through quaint hamlets, rolling meadows, and panoramic passes.

- 📍 *Start*: Almaty
- 🗺 *Route*: Almaty → Kegen → Saty → Charyn Canyon

- 🏔 *Stopover*: Stay overnight at an eco-yurt in Saty
- 🌐 More Info: kazakhstan.travel/nature/charyn

🏛 Bozzhyra Valley – The Martian Route

Located in Mangystau, this off-road route through chalky cliffs and stone spires looks like another planet. The **Bozzhyra "fangs"** are Instagram-famous, but getting there is an adventure.

- 🚗 *4WD Required*: Yes
- 🛑 *Tip*: Hire a local guide from Aktau or Shetpe
- 📷 *Don't Miss*: Sunrise on the plateau
- 🌐 Explore: mangystau.travel

⛰ Zailiysky Alatau Alpine Drive

Craving alpine scenery? Drive from Almaty up to Big Almaty Lake and onward toward the **Zailiysky Alatau Mountains**. This road offers stunning switchbacks and glacier views, especially in late spring.

- 🏔 *Highlight*: Big Almaty Lake ⬜
- 🛑 *Altitude*: 2,500m

- ☼ *Best Time*: May–October
- 🌐 More Info: kazakhstan.travel/nature/big-almaty-lake

🌿 Steppe Crossing: Astana to Pavlodar

This lesser-traveled northern route lets you experience the **Kazakh steppe in its purest form** — a surreal drive with eagles soaring above and nomadic herders in the distance.

- 📍 *Route*: Astana → Kokshetau → Pavlodar
- ⛰ *Camp Tip*: Stop at Shchuchinsk Lake for a peaceful overnight

Unusual Attractions Worth Visiting

Kazakhstan has no shortage of strange and surprising places — from quirky museums to spiritual anomalies and geological oddities. Here are a few fascinating detours:

🎻 Museum of Broken Relationships – Almaty Edition

A satellite branch of the famous Croatian museum, this heartfelt and sometimes hilarious collection of love stories and personal relics is tucked inside an arts center in Almaty.

- 📍 *Location*: 44 Tulebayev Street, Almaty

- 🕐 *Open*: Tue–Sun, 10am–6pm
- 🌐 Website: brokenships.com

🪐 Kosmodrome Tour – Baikonur Launch Site

More than just rockets — this is a chance to walk in the footsteps of **Gagarin**. See launch pads, Soviet-era control rooms, and the Museum of the Cosmodrome. A special permit is required.

- 📍 *Location*: Baikonur, Kyzylorda Region
- 🚀 *Tip*: Plan 2 months in advance for permits
- 🌐 Info: roscosmos.ru

💀 Valley of Balls (Torysh Valley)

One of nature's strangest landscapes — hundreds of **perfectly round stone spheres** scattered across a desert plain. Locals say they're the frozen remains of a legendary battle.

- 📍 *Location*: Mangystau Region
- 📷 *Photography Tip*: Visit during golden hour
- 🌐 Read More: mangystau.travel

🕳 Underground Mosques of Beket-Ata and Shakpak-Ata

These holy shrines are carved into caves and cliffs — used by Sufi mystics and pilgrims for centuries. Deep silence, candlelit chambers, and a sense of timelessness await.

- 📍 *Location*: Mangystau Region
- 🙏 *Tip*: Dress modestly and remove shoes before entering
- 🌐 Details: kazakhstan.travel/spiritual-sites

🍬 Center of Eurasia Monument – Nur-Sultan

A strange sculpture marks the supposed **exact center of the Eurasian continent**. It's quirky, obscure, and oddly compelling — and makes for a fun photo stop.

- 📍 *Location*: Nur-Sultan (near city outskirts)
- 📷 *Best For*: Geo-curiosity lovers

🧭 Travel Tip:

For remote spots like Mangystau, Torysh, or Beket-Ata, always carry water, offline maps, and **local SIM cards** for emergency contact. Most of these areas are **unreachable by public transport** — a rented 4x4 or guided tour is essential.

Chapter 7

Food and Drink

Kazakhstan's culinary landscape is a bold fusion of **nomadic traditions, Central Asian flavors, and Soviet influences**. Eating here is not just about nourishment—it's a full cultural experience. Whether you're dining in a high-end restaurant or sharing a meal in a village yurt, Kazakh hospitality shines through every bite. From tender horse meat delicacies to sizzling street snacks, here's your ultimate guide to eating your way across Kazakhstan.

Must-Try Local Dishes and Where to Find Them

Kazakh cuisine reflects its **nomadic heritage**, favoring meat (especially horse and lamb), dairy, and hearty grains. Meals are often communal, and guests are treated with reverence. Below are iconic dishes every traveler should taste—plus exactly where to find them.

🍲 Beshbarmak (Бешбармак) – "Five Fingers"

The national dish of Kazakhstan, *Beshbarmak* is made of **boiled meat (usually horse or lamb)** served over wide noodles with a rich onion broth. Traditionally eaten by hand, it's a symbol of Kazakh unity and celebration.

- 🥄 *Try it at*:
  - **Rumi Restaurant**, Almaty – rumi.kz
  - **Qazaq Gourmet**, Nur-Sultan – qazaqgourmet.kz
- 💡 *Tip*: Ask for "kazı" (horse meat sausage) for an authentic experience.

🍳 Kuyrdak (Куырдак) – Offal Stew

A rich, flavorful dish made with liver, kidneys, heart, and onions, *Kuyrdak* is deeply traditional and beloved across rural Kazakhstan.

- 🥄 *Best in*:
  - **EthnoVillage "Huns"**, near Almaty – ethnovillage.kz
  - **Local homestays** in Shymkent and Turkestan

🥟 Manti (Манты) – Steamed Dumplings

Large dumplings stuffed with **minced meat (lamb/beef), onions, and spices**, often steamed and served with sour cream or butter.

- 🍴 *Try it at*:
  - ○ **Line Brew**, Almaty – linebrew.kz
  - ○ **Navat Cafe**, Nur-Sultan – navat.kz

🍢 Shashlik (Шашлык) – Meat Skewers

A Central Asian BBQ favorite, *Shashlik* is marinated meat grilled over coals and often served with raw onions and vinegar.

- 🍴 *Best street spots*:
  - ○ **Green Bazaar**, Almaty
  - ○ **Shashlychnaya #1**, Shymkent

🍲 Plov (Плов) – Central Asian Rice Pilaf

Saffron rice cooked with carrots, garlic, and lamb. A staple across Central Asia, each region has its own twist.

- 🍴 *Try it at*:

- o **Uzbek-themed restaurants** in Turkestan or Taraz
- o **Alasha Restaurant**, Almaty – alasha.kz

🥛 Kymyz (Қымыз) – Fermented Mare's Milk

A fermented, slightly sour and bubbly drink made from horse milk. It's an acquired taste, but a **must-try traditional beverage**.

- • 📍 *Best in*:
  - o Villages around **Saty**, **Karkaraly**, or **Nura**
  - o Summer festivals and roadside stalls

Street Food Scene

Kazakhstan's street food is flavorful, fast, and surprisingly diverse, blending Soviet snacks, Central Asian bites, and modern café fare. Wander through local markets and bazaars to sample the very best.

🥟 Samsa (Самса)

Flaky, oven-baked pastries filled with minced lamb or beef, onions, and sometimes pumpkin. Often cooked in a *tandoor oven*.

- 📍 *Where to find*:
  - ○ **Green Bazaar**, Almaty
  - ○ **Central Market**, Shymkent

🥟 Baursak (Баурсаки) – Fried Bread Balls

Soft, golden doughnuts served with tea—often seen at markets, weddings, and roadside stands.

- 📍 *Where to find*:
  - ○ Tea houses across Almaty
  - ○ Rural food stalls during **Nauryz (Spring Festival)**

🧃 Shubat (Шұбат) – Camel Milk

Creamier and slightly milder than *kymyz*, this fermented camel milk is rich in nutrients and probiotics.

- 📍 *Try it at*:
  - ○ **Astana Market (Artyom Bazaar)**
  - ○ **Kyzylorda Region** for authentic desert-style versions

🍞 Lagman (Лагман) – Hand-Pulled Noodles

A Uyghur-Chinese fusion dish of stir-fried beef and vegetables over hand-pulled noodles. Savory, spicy, and immensely satisfying.

- 🥄 *Try it at*:
    - **Uyghur cafes in Almaty**
    - **Dungan restaurants**, Karakol area (near Kyrgyz border)

🍰 Soviet-Era Desserts

From *Bird's Milk Cake* to *Zefir (fruit marshmallow)*, Kazakhstan's Soviet sweet tooth lives on.

- 🥄 *Where to find*:
    - **Café Central**, Nur-Sultan
    - **Confectionery sections in Magnum supermarkets**

🍲 Foodie Tip:

Kazakh meals are often accompanied by **black tea or green tea**, and guests are expected to drink at least three cups. Refusing can be seen as rude in more traditional settings.

Best Restaurants and Cafés

Kazakhstan's culinary scene is rapidly evolving. While traditional Kazakh meals remain staples, cities like **Almaty** and **Astana (Nur-Sultan)** now offer a vibrant mix of fine dining, hipster cafés, and international cuisines. Whether you crave a gourmet dinner, a cup of artisan coffee, or a relaxed brunch, here are the top places to savor.

🏙 Almaty

1. Gakku Restaurant – Traditional Kazakh in an Elegant Setting

📍 *Dostyk Ave 183, Almaty*

🌐 gakku.kz

☎ +7 727 225 22 88

Enjoy beautifully plated Kazakh meals like *beshbarmak*, *kuurdak*, and *kazı* in a fine-dining atmosphere. Live folk music adds a cultural touch.

2. Café Central – European & Kazakh Fusion

📍 *Tole Bi Street 56, Almaty*

🌐 cafecentral.kz

☕ Try their breakfast sets and homemade cakes. A perfect brunch spot near Panfilov Park.

3. Traveler's Coffee – Cozy Café for Digital Nomads

📍 Multiple branches across Almaty

🌐 travelerscoffee.kz

🧖 Free Wi-Fi, English-speaking staff, and great cappuccinos make this a remote worker's dream.

🏛 Astana (Nur-Sultan)

1. Qazaq Gourmet – Refined Kazakh Cuisine

📍 *Mangilik El Ave, Astana*

🌐 qazaqgourmet.kz

🍾 A luxurious space to experience the nation's finest dishes, served with theatrical flair.

2. Del Papa – Italian Elegance in the Capital

📍 *Kabanbay Batyr Ave 45A, Astana*

🌐 delpapa.kz

☕ Authentic pasta, seafood, and a romantic ambiance make this a favorite among locals and expats.

3. Rumi – Persian Central Asian Cuisine

📍 *Syganak St 29, Astana*

🌐 rumi.kz

🏤 A blend of Kazakh and Persian flavors with stunning interior inspired by ancient Silk Road motifs.

🏔️ Other Cities & Hidden Gems

1. Alasha Restaurant – Shymkent

📍 *Zhibek Zholy, Shymkent*

🌐 alasha.kz

🏛️ Eat in traditional yurts with folk performances while enjoying *lagman* and grilled meats.

2. Otrar Café – Turkestan

📍 *Near Hazrat Sultan Mosque*

🏠 A peaceful stopover for travelers visiting the UNESCO sites. Try their *plov* and *shubat*.

3. Yurt Café – Karakol (on the border near Kyrgyzstan)

📍 *Valikhanov Street, Karakol*

⬡ Cozy up in a heated yurt with hot tea and grilled samsas during mountain treks.

Local Beverages and Nightlife

Kazakhstan's drinking culture is subtle but rich. While Islamic traditions may restrict alcohol in rural areas, **urban nightlife thrives** with craft beer pubs, cocktail lounges, and traditional beverage spots.

Traditional Beverages

1. Kymyz (Қымыз) – Fermented Mare's Milk

- Slightly tangy, probiotic-rich, and symbolic of Kazakh hospitality.
- 📍 Best enjoyed in **Almaty region villages** or local markets like *Green Bazaar*.

2. Shubat (Шұбат) – Camel Milk

- Creamier than kymyz and popular in the western steppe regions.
- 📍 Common in **Kyzylorda** and *Aral Sea* regions.
- Served chilled at yurt cafes and traditional gatherings.

3. Ayran (Айран) – Yogurt Drink

- A cool, salty yogurt drink perfect for hot days.
- Available in every restaurant, and especially during *Nauryz* festivities.

Nightlife Hotspots

Almaty has the liveliest scene, with bars and lounges open until late. **Astana** is more sleek and modern, with rooftop lounges and jazz bars.

🏙 Almaty Nightlife

1. The Shakespeare Pub

📍 *Shevchenko St 59, Almaty*

🌐 shakespeare.kz

🍺 Cozy English pub with local beers and classic pub food. Friendly for tourists.

2. Line Brew

📍 *Furmanov Ave 187, Almaty*

🌐 linebrew.kz

🥩 Steakhouse and brewery combo with a medieval castle theme. Great place to try Kazakh craft beers.

3. Sky Lounge Bar – High-Rise Glamour

📍 *Esentai Tower, Almaty*

🌐 skylounge.kz

🍸 Rooftop cocktails with panoramic views of the Tien Shan mountains.

🏙️ Astana (Nur-Sultan) Nightlife

1. The Barley

📍 *Turan Ave, Astana*

🌐 barley.kz

🎷 Live music, chic atmosphere, and premium drink selections.

2. Versus Club

📍 *Saryarka Ave 10/1*

🎧 Electronic music, dance floors, and popular among young Kazakhs.

3. Chukotka Bar

📍 *Kabanbay Batyr Ave*

🎲 Underground vibe with retro decor. Expect poetry nights and DJ sets.

ⓘ Nightlife Tips

- 🔞 Legal drinking age is **21**.

- 🚕 Use **Yandex Go** or **inDrive** for safe transport at night.

- 🍸 Alcohol is **not widely consumed** in rural areas—respect local norms.

- 👗 Dress code: Casual-smart in lounges, upscale for fine dining.

Food Etiquette and Tips for Eating Safely

Kazakhstan's food culture is deeply rooted in **hospitality**, **tradition**, and **respect**. Understanding local etiquette and following a few safety tips will enhance your culinary experience—especially when dining in someone's home, trying street food, or visiting rural areas.

🫓 Kazakh Food Etiquette: Dining with Respect

1. Respect the Elders 👴

When dining with locals, always let the eldest or most respected guest begin eating first. It's customary to serve them first and allow them to give a short blessing.

2. Hands Matter ✋

Traditionally, meals—especially *beshbarmak*—may be eaten with hands during family or yurt gatherings. Wash your hands before and after meals. Use your right hand when eating or giving/receiving food.

3. Bread is Sacred 🍞

Bread (*nan*) is never wasted. Avoid placing it upside down or throwing it away. In rural homes, leftover bread is often set aside respectfully for animals or the earth.

4. Don't Decline Tea! ☕

Tea (*shai*) is a big part of Kazakh hospitality. It's polite to accept at least one small cup, even if you're not thirsty. Hosts may keep topping up your cup—if you've had enough, leave a small amount in the cup.

5. Sharing is Caring 👪

Meals are often communal, especially in rural homes. Dishes are shared, and it's polite to taste everything offered to you, even in small amounts.

6. Remove Shoes at the Door 👟

In homes and traditional restaurants with carpeted floors or low seating, removing your shoes at the entrance is expected.

☑ Tips for Eating Safely in Kazakhstan

While food hygiene is generally good in major cities, rural areas and open markets require some extra caution. Here are essential safety tips:

🌀 Cleanliness & Preparation

- **Drink bottled water** 💧 – Tap water is not potable in most places. Always buy sealed bottles or bring a filter bottle.
- **Avoid ice cubes** in local drinks unless you're at a reputable café or hotel.
- **Wash fruits** 🍈 with bottled or boiled water before eating them raw.
- **Eat at busy stalls** – High customer turnover often means fresher food.

🍪 Street Food Safety

Kazakhstan's street food is tempting—samsa, shashlik, and baursak are must-tries—but follow these tips:

- 🌡 **Check food temperature** – Hot foods should be steaming, cold foods well chilled.
- ✋ **Observe hygiene** – Choose vendors who wear gloves and maintain clean stalls.
- 🚫 **Skip raw meat** – Avoid dishes with undercooked meats or raw fish outside of upscale establishments.

💊 Traveler's Digestive Health

- 💊 Bring **antacids and anti-diarrhea medication**, just in case.
- 🥛 Try **fermented drinks** like kymyz or shubat gradually—they may upset unaccustomed stomachs.
- 🥛 **Lactose intolerance** is rare in locals, but if you're sensitive, ask for dairy-free options (*bez moloka* in Russian: "без молока").

🌿 Halal and Vegetarian Considerations

- 🕌 **Halal food** is widely available, especially in rural and Muslim-majority areas.
- 🎍 **Vegetarians/Vegans** should inquire clearly (*bez myasa* = "no meat")—many dishes contain hidden meat or broth. In cities like Almaty and Astana, you'll find international restaurants with veg-friendly menus.

📝 Useful Phrases for Eating Out

- "I don't eat meat" – *Я не ем мясо* (Ya nye yem myasa)
- "Is this halal?" – *Это халяль?* (Eto khalyal?)
- "No onions, please" – *Без лука, пожалуйста* (Bez luka, pozhaluysta)
- "Can I have it less spicy?" – *Можно не остро?* (Mozhno ne ostro?)

With these etiquette insights and food safety tips, you're ready to eat confidently across Kazakhstan's rich culinary landscape. 🍽️🥢

Chapter 8

Culture and Traditions

Kazakhstan is a country where ancient nomadic traditions blend seamlessly with modern lifestyles. The heart of Central Asia, it boasts a diverse cultural landscape shaped by Turkic roots, Soviet legacy, Islamic influence, and a resilient spirit that lives on in its people. In this chapter, we explore the depth of Kazakhstan's cultural heritage and provide a guide to understanding and respectfully engaging with local customs.

History and Heritage

Kazakhstan's history is a rich tapestry woven from millennia of nomadic life, empires, and evolving identities. Once home to ancient Silk Road cities and Mongol khans, Kazakhstan has seen the rise and fall of powerful steppe kingdoms and was a key player in Central Asian geopolitics long before its Soviet chapter.

📜 A Brief Historical Overview

- **Early Nomadic Tribes**: For centuries, Kazakh ancestors roamed the vast steppes, living in yurts, herding livestock, and practicing animism and Tengriism (sky worship).

- **The Kazakh Khanate** (15th century): Marked the beginning of a unified Kazakh identity, ruled by khans and guided by customary laws (*adat*).

- **Russian Imperial Era**: By the 18th and 19th centuries, Russia began incorporating Kazakh lands into its empire, introducing new governance and Orthodox Christian influence.

- **Soviet Kazakhstan**: Under Soviet rule (1920s–1991), Kazakhstan underwent forced collectivization, witnessed the devastating famine of the 1930s, and became a nuclear test site. The USSR also relocated ethnic groups here, creating the multi-ethnic society seen today.

- **Independence (1991–Present)**: Following the Soviet collapse, Kazakhstan declared independence on **December 16, 1991**, and has since embraced economic reform, nation-building, and global diplomacy.

📍 Recommended Historical Sites to Visit:

- **State Historical Museum** – Almaty
  🕐 10:00 AM – 5:00 PM (closed Mondays)

📍 Address: 44 Samal-1, Almaty

🔗 Visit Website

- **Ethno-Memorial Complex "Map of Kazakhstan – Atameken"** – Astana

A miniature open-air map showcasing landmarks and regions.

📍 Address: Qabanbay Batyr Ave 4, Astana

📞 +7 7172 55 64 63

Local Customs and Etiquette

Kazakh customs are rooted in **respect, generosity, and hospitality**, making travelers feel welcomed across urban and rural communities. Understanding a few key traditions will help you engage warmly and avoid cultural missteps.

Hospitality is Sacred

The Kazakh saying *"Konak keldi – qut keldi"* ("A guest brings blessings") speaks volumes about their approach to visitors. Whether you're in a remote village or a city home, expect to be treated as an honored guest, often with tea, snacks, and heartfelt conversation.

💬 **Tip**: Accepting tea, even just a few sips, is a respectful gesture. Declining it may be considered impolite.

👪 Respect for Elders

Elders are deeply respected. In group settings, stand when an elder enters, greet them first, and always offer them the best seat or first serving. Use formal titles like *Aga* (older brother) or *Apa* (older sister) as a sign of respect.

🕊 Greetings and Social Norms

- A common greeting: *Salemetsiz be?* (Hello – formal)
- A handshake is standard between men, but avoid initiating one with women unless they offer first.
- Placing your right hand over your heart while nodding is a respectful, non-contact way to greet someone.

🕌 Religion and Modesty

Kazakhstan is secular but has a Muslim majority. Islam influences many social norms:

- Dress modestly when visiting religious or rural areas. Long skirts/pants and covered shoulders are appreciated.

- During **Ramadan**, avoid eating or drinking in public out of courtesy in conservative areas.
- Remove shoes before entering mosques or traditional homes.

🏠 Inside a Kazakh Home

- Remove your shoes at the door.
- Bring a small gift (fruit, sweets, or flowers) if invited.
- Complimenting the home or food is a kind gesture.
- Meals are often shared from a central dish. Only use your right hand for eating or passing food.

🏛️ Cultural Events & Festivals

Kazakhstan's cultural calendar is filled with colorful festivals celebrating its heritage, seasons, and ethnic diversity.

🎊 Major Celebrations:

- **Nauryz (March 21–23)** – The Persian New Year and spring equinox. Expect vibrant street festivals, *beshbarmak* feasts, music, and traditional sports like *Kyz Kuu* (horseback courtship games).

📍 Best Celebrated In: Almaty, Turkistan, and rural villages.

- **Constitution Day (August 30)** – Patriotic parades and concerts nationwide.
- **Unity Day (May 1)** – Highlights Kazakhstan's 130+ ethnic groups with traditional clothing, dance, and cuisine.
- **Independence Day (December 16)** – Marked with fireworks, cultural exhibitions, and tributes to Kazakhstan's history.

🔗 Full Festival Calendar

Understanding and respecting these customs will open doors—literally and figuratively. Kazakhs appreciate travelers who show curiosity and kindness toward their traditions. Be open, respectful, and you'll walk away with stories and friendships to last a lifetime.

Festivals and Celebrations

Kazakhstan is a country that celebrates its diversity, rich cultural heritage, and the changing seasons with vibrant festivals and joyful events. Whether you're visiting in winter, spring, summer, or fall, there's always something exciting happening, from ancient traditions to modern celebrations. These festivals give you the chance to immerse yourself in the heart of Kazakh culture and share in the country's sense of community and togetherness.

Key Festivals and Celebrations

1. Nauryz (March 21–23)

Nauryz, the Persian New Year, is the most significant and widely celebrated festival in Kazakhstan. It marks the arrival of spring and symbolizes renewal, fertility, and harmony with nature. Celebrated across the country, it's an exuberant festival featuring folk music, traditional dances, and public feasts with *beshbarmak* (Kazakh national dish) served in abundance.

- **Highlights**: Street parades, equestrian games, traditional singing, and dance performances.
- **Where to Celebrate**: Almaty, Astana, Turkistan, and rural areas.
- **Traditional Foods**: *Nauryz kozhe* (a ceremonial soup made with seven ingredients), *baursak*, and *shashlik*.

2. Kazakh Independence Day (December 16–17)

This is a patriotic holiday to honor Kazakhstan's independence from the Soviet Union, which was declared in 1991. It is celebrated with state ceremonies, fireworks, and cultural exhibitions that showcase the country's proud history and achievements.

- **Highlights**: Fireworks, national pride parades, and concerts.
- **Where to Celebrate**: Nationwide, with major celebrations in Almaty and Astana.

3. Republic Day (December 16)

Republic Day commemorates the day Kazakhstan adopted its first constitution. It's a day of national pride, with various events that highlight the unity and sovereignty of the country.

- **Highlights**: Flag-raising ceremonies, cultural shows, and exhibitions.
- **Where to Celebrate**: Almaty, Astana, and other major cities.

4. Kymyz Festival (August)

This lesser-known but fascinating festival celebrates *kymyz*, the traditional fermented mare's milk, a drink with centuries-old significance among Kazakh nomads. The festival includes tasting events, cooking competitions, and horse riding contests.

- **Highlights**: *Kymyz* tasting, horseback riding, and traditional music.
- **Where to Celebrate**: Mostly in rural areas and traditional nomadic camps.

5. Kurban Ait (Islamic Festival)

Kurban Ait is an important Islamic holiday where Kazakhs make sacrifices and share meals with the less fortunate. The festival is marked by prayers in mosques and large gatherings where food is shared among family and community members.

- **Highlights**: Community prayers, charity work, and feasts.
- **Where to Celebrate**: Throughout Kazakhstan, especially in Muslim-majority regions.

6. Astana Day (July 6)

Astana (now known as Nur-Sultan) is the capital of Kazakhstan, and Astana Day marks the city's transformation from a small provincial town to the country's dynamic and modern capital. The day is celebrated with grand parades, fireworks, and cultural performances.

- **Highlights**: Parades, fireworks, and concerts.
- **Where to Celebrate**: Nur-Sultan (Astana).

🎧 Music, Dance, and Traditions

Kazakh festivals often feature traditional music performances, with the sound of the *dombra* (a two-stringed instrument) and *kobyz* (a stringed instrument played with a bow) echoing through the air. Dance is an integral part of celebrations, with group dances and performances often representing the various ethnic groups that make up Kazakhstan's diverse population. Whether at a public festival or a private gathering, Kazakhs enjoy music that spans centuries and is still very much a part of their daily lives.

Dress Codes and Social Norms

Kazakhstan's dress codes and social norms are influenced by a mix of traditional Kazakh culture and modern global trends. However, there are a few important aspects to keep in mind to ensure you respect the local customs and blend in appropriately.

Dress Codes for Men and Women

1. Traditional Clothing

Traditional Kazakh attire is worn on special occasions like weddings, holidays, and festivals. For men, this includes a *shapan* (long coat), *kalpak* (traditional hat), and *jubba* (robe). Women wear long dresses or skirts, often adorned with intricate patterns, and headscarves are common.

- **For Men**: When dressing in formal settings, men may wear a suit, but casual wear like jeans and a shirt is also acceptable. It's important to avoid overly revealing clothing in rural areas.

- **For Women**: Modesty is appreciated, especially in more conservative settings. Women often wear dresses or skirts that cover the knees, and it's advisable to cover the shoulders as well. In urban areas, you'll see a mix of modern and traditional dress.

2. Modesty

Kazakhstan is a Muslim-majority country, and while it's not as conservative as some other parts of Central Asia, modesty is still important. When visiting religious sites or rural areas, it's essential to dress modestly, covering arms and legs. In mosques, both men and women are required to cover their heads.

- **Men**: When visiting a mosque, men should cover their heads and remove shoes before entering.
- **Women**: In mosques and some rural areas, women are expected to cover their heads with a scarf or shawl.

3. Casual Wear in Cities

In major cities like Almaty and Nur-Sultan, the dress code is more relaxed and globalized. Here, you'll see a mix of modern Western clothing and stylish attire, and wearing jeans, skirts, and dresses in urban areas is common.

However, during the winter months, heavy coats, scarves, and gloves are a necessity due to the cold temperatures.

Social Etiquette and Manners

Kazakh social etiquette is rooted in hospitality and respect. Here's a guide to help you navigate social situations:

1. Greetings

- The traditional Kazakh greeting is a handshake, though men and women may not always shake hands, especially if the woman is older. It's polite to bow your head slightly while shaking hands with an elder.
- When greeting someone, it's customary to ask about their health and well-being. A simple *"Salemetsiz be?"* (Hello) is sufficient, but showing genuine interest in the person is valued.

2. Respect for Elders

As with most Central Asian cultures, Kazakh people deeply respect their elders. Always greet them first in group settings, stand when they enter the room, and offer them the best seat at the table.

3. Gift Giving

Bringing a gift is a sign of respect, especially when visiting someone's home. Gifts don't have to be extravagant; fruit, sweets, or a small souvenir from your country are appreciated. Avoid giving knives, scissors, or sharp objects, as they symbolize cutting ties.

4. Table Manners

- When eating, it's considered polite to wait for the eldest to begin before you start your meal.
- Use your right hand for eating, passing food, or shaking hands.
- It's also customary to finish everything on your plate as a sign of appreciation.

Kazakhstan's cultural fabric is as vast and varied as the country's landscapes, and understanding these key customs and traditions will help you immerse yourself in the country's spirit while showing respect for its people and values.

Language Basics and Key Phrases

Kazakhstan is a multilingual country, with Kazakh and Russian being the two official languages. Kazakh is the state language and is widely spoken in rural areas, while Russian is more commonly used in urban centers and is the predominant language in business and government. English is not widely spoken outside major tourist destinations, so having a few key phrases in Kazakh or Russian can help you navigate more easily and make a positive impression with locals.

🏠 Kazakh Language Basics

Kazakh is a Turkic language with its own alphabet, though it has switched from Cyrillic to the Latin script in recent years. While Kazakh is commonly spoken in rural areas, it is important to know that Russian is still dominant in cities like Almaty and Nur-Sultan. Here are a few basic phrases in Kazakh to help you communicate:

1. Greetings

- **Hello** – *Salemetsiz be?* (Сәлеметсіз бе?)
- **Good morning** – *Kün tüdí* (Күн түсті)
- **Good evening** – *Kün tünygen* (Күн түніген)
- **Goodbye** – *Sau bol* (Сау бол)

- **How are you?** – *Qalai jazdy?* (Қалай жазды?)
- **I'm fine, thank you** – *Jaqsy, ráhmét* (Жақсы, рақмет)

2. Common Phrases

- **Please** – *Öte* (Өте)
- **Thank you** – *Ráhmét* (Рақмет)
- **Yes** – *Iya* (Иә)
- **No** – *Jok* (Жоқ)
- **Excuse me** – *Keshiriniz* (Кешіріңіз)
- **Sorry** – *Kechirińiz* (Кешіріңіз)
- **I don't understand** – *Men túsinbeymin* (Мен түсінбеймін)
- **Can you help me?** – *Meni kómektesip jiberesińiz be?* (Менің көмектесіп жібересіз бе?)

3. Numbers

- **One** – *Birinshi* (Бірінші)
- **Two** – *Eki* (Екі)
- **Three** – *Úsh* (Үш)
- **Four** – *Tórt* (Төрт)
- **Five** – *Bies* (Бес)
- **Ten** – *On* (Он)

RU Russian Language Basics

Russian is more commonly spoken in Kazakhstan's major cities, particularly in areas with higher concentrations of Russian speakers. It's a Slavic language and uses the Cyrillic script. Here are some basic Russian phrases to help you when navigating urban environments:

1. Greetings

- **Hello** – *Zdravstvuyte* (Здравствуйте)
- **Good morning** – *Dobroye utro* (Доброе утро)
- **Good evening** – *Dobryy vecher* (Добрый вечер)
- **Goodbye** – *Do svidaniya* (До свидания)
- **How are you?** – *Kak dela?* (Как дела?)
- **I'm fine, thank you** – *Khorosho, spasibo* (Хорошо, спасибо)

2. Common Phrases

- **Please** – *Pozhaluysta* (Пожалуйста)
- **Thank you** – *Spasibo* (Спасибо)
- **Yes** – *Da* (Да)
- **No** – *Net* (Нет)
- **Excuse me** – *Izvinite* (Извините)
- **Sorry** – *Proshu proshcheniya* (Прошу прощения)
- **I don't understand** – *Ya ne ponimayu* (Я не понимаю)

- **Can you help me?** – *Mozhete mne pomoch'?* (Можете мне помочь?)

3. Numbers

- **One** – *Odin* (Один)
- **Two** – *Dva* (Два)
- **Three** – *Tree* (Три)
- **Four** – *Chetyre* (Четыре)
- **Five** – *Pyat'* (Пять)
- **Ten** – *Desyat'* (Десять)

◉ English Phrases

While English is becoming increasingly popular, especially among younger generations and in tourist areas, it's not universally spoken in rural areas. If you're traveling to more remote locations, knowing a few key phrases in Kazakh or Russian can be very useful. Here are a few basic English phrases that might come in handy:

- **Where is the nearest hotel?** – *Gde nakhoditsya blizhayshiy otel'?* (Где находится ближайший отель?)

- **How much does this cost?** – *Skol'ko eto stoit?* (Сколько это стоит?)

- **I'm lost. Can you help me?** – *Ya zabloshchilsya. Mozhete pomoch'?* (Я заблудился. Можете помочь?)

- **Where is the nearest restaurant?** – *Gde nakhoditsya blizhayshiy restoran?* (Где находится ближайший ресторан?)

Helpful Tips for Communication

- **Use Simple Language**: When speaking in either Kazakh or Russian, try to use simple and clear language, as most people are not fluent in English.

- **Learn the Cyrillic Alphabet**: If you're planning to travel to cities where Russian is widely spoken, learning the Cyrillic alphabet can help you read signs, menus, and directions more easily.

- **Use Translation Apps**: If you're not confident with your language skills, apps like Google Translate can assist in translating signs and phrases, helping you communicate with locals more effectively.

- **Be Patient**: Locals may not speak perfect English, but they are generally friendly and will appreciate any effort to speak their language.

With these language basics and key phrases, you'll have a much easier time navigating Kazakhstan's diverse cultural landscape. Whether you're conversing with locals in Kazakh, Russian, or English, being able to communicate will enhance your experience and bring you closer to the heart of Kazakhstan.

Chapter 9

Shopping and Souvenirs

Kazakhstan offers a rich shopping experience that blends modern retail with traditional craftsmanship. From bustling markets in the heart of Almaty to charming handicraft stalls in local towns, there is a wealth of unique finds that can serve as reminders of your journey. In this chapter, we will explore some of the best places to shop in Kazakhstan, as well as the most authentic souvenirs to bring home.

Popular Local Markets and Shopping Streets

Kazakhstan's markets are an essential part of its cultural fabric. These places not only offer goods but also provide a glimpse into the country's way of life. Here are the most popular markets and shopping streets that every traveler should visit:

1. Zelyony Bazaar (Green Bazaar), Almaty

- **Location**: Zelyony Bazaar, Almaty, Kazakhstan

- **Description**: Located in the heart of Almaty, Zelyony Bazaar is a vibrant market where locals come to buy fresh produce, spices, herbs, and traditional foods. The market's atmosphere is a mix of old and new, with vendors selling everything from dried fruits to handmade textiles. It's also a great place to try local treats like *shashlik* (grilled meat skewers) and *chak-chak* (honey dessert).
- **Contact**: You can reach out to the Almaty Tourism Board for more information on visiting hours or events at visit.almaty.kz 🌐.

2. Tsum Shopping Mall, Almaty

- **Location**: 80 Al-Farabi Avenue, Almaty, Kazakhstan
- **Description**: For those who prefer modern shopping, Tsum Mall is the place to go. Offering a wide variety of luxury goods, clothing, and international brands, this shopping center is a popular destination for both locals and tourists. It also has a range of restaurants and cafes, making it the perfect spot for a relaxing shopping experience.
- **Contact**: Visit their official website at tsum.kz 🌐 for more details on hours and special promotions.

3. Arbat Street, Almaty

- **Location**: Arbat Street, Almaty, Kazakhstan
- **Description**: This pedestrian-friendly street is known for its lively atmosphere, street performers, and local art galleries. Strolling down Arbat Street offers the chance to explore boutique shops selling handmade goods, jewelry, clothing, and more. It's a great place to find unique Kazakh fashion, traditional items, and artistic souvenirs.
- **Opening Hours**: Shops usually open from 10:00 AM – 8:00 PM.

4. Shymbulak Ski Resort Market

- **Location**: Shymbulak Ski Resort, Almaty Region, Kazakhstan
- **Description**: For something truly unique, head to the Shymbulak Ski Resort, where you'll find small shops selling local handicrafts, warm clothing, and souvenirs related to mountain sports. It's also a good spot for picking up winter gear and accessories to take home.
- **Opening Hours**: Open daily during the ski season from 9:00 AM – 7:00 PM.

5. Bazaar of Kyzylorda

- **Location**: Kyzylorda, Kazakhstan
- **Description**: If you're traveling through the southern regions of Kazakhstan, make sure to stop by the Kyzylorda Bazaar. Known for its colorful stalls and rich selection of local items, the market offers everything from fresh fruit to handmade pottery and textiles. It's also an ideal place to find Kazakh-style carpets, felt items, and traditional jewelry.

Authentic Souvenirs to Bring Home

Kazakhstan's diverse culture and rich history offer plenty of opportunities to purchase beautiful and meaningful souvenirs. Whether you're looking for something for yourself or a gift for someone back home, here are some authentic items you should consider:

1. Kazakh Rugs and Carpets

- **Description**: Known for their intricate designs and vibrant colors, Kazakh rugs and carpets are one of the most coveted souvenirs. Made with wool and often featuring traditional patterns such as geometric shapes, floral motifs, or animal symbols, they are perfect for bringing a piece of Kazakh artistry into your home.

- **Where to Buy**: Zelyony Bazaar in Almaty and local artisan markets in rural towns.

2. Shyrdaks (Felt Rugs)

- **Description**: These traditional felt rugs are crafted from sheep's wool and dyed with natural colors. The patterns vary from region to region, and each design holds significance within the Kazakh culture. Shyrdaks are a symbol of nomadic life and make for a beautiful and authentic souvenir.
- **Where to Buy**: Arbat Street in Almaty or directly from local artisans in rural areas.

3. Kazakh Jewelry

- **Description**: Handcrafted jewelry is another highlight of Kazakh culture. You'll find unique pieces made from silver, with designs inspired by Kazakh traditions and nature. Look for intricate necklaces, bracelets, earrings, and rings that feature traditional symbols like eagles, horses, and stars.

- **Where to Buy**: Markets in Almaty, particularly Arbat Street, and jewelry shops in major cities.

4. Kazakh Musical Instruments

- **Description**: For a truly unique souvenir, consider purchasing a traditional Kazakh musical instrument like the *dombra* (a two-stringed instrument) or the *kobyz* (a bowed string instrument). These instruments are deeply rooted in Kazakhstan's nomadic culture and make for an intriguing and educational gift.
- **Where to Buy**: Specialist stores in Almaty or from local artisans.

5. Kazakh Tea and Teapots

- **Description**: Kazakh tea culture is an important part of daily life, with green and black tea being popular throughout the country. You can buy loose-leaf tea to bring home, along with beautifully designed teapots and tea cups. These items often come in traditional styles, reflecting the country's artistic heritage.

- **Where to Buy**: Zelyony Bazaar, local markets, and high-end shops in major cities.

6. Traditional Kazakh Clothing

- **Description**: Kazakh clothing often features bright colors and intricate embroidery. You can purchase items such as *shapan* (traditional robes), felt hats, scarves, and gloves. These items are often made from wool, cotton, or silk and are a great way to remember the country's heritage.
- **Where to Buy**: Almaty's Arbat Street or craft markets in rural areas.

7. Kazakh Leather Goods

- **Description**: Leather items such as wallets, belts, and bags are common souvenirs and are often hand-stitched and decorated with Kazakh motifs. These high-quality products make excellent gifts and will last for years to come.
- **Where to Buy**: Zelyony Bazaar in Almaty or local leather artisans throughout the country.

🛍 Shopping Tips in Kazakhstan

- **Bargaining**: Bargaining is common in local markets, so don't hesitate to negotiate prices, especially in open-air bazaars.
- **Currency**: The local currency is the Kazakhstani tenge (KZT). Be sure to carry some local currency when shopping at markets or small shops, as credit cards may not always be accepted.
- **Tax-Free Shopping**: Kazakhstan offers a tax-free shopping program for foreign tourists. Be sure to ask about it when making larger purchases, especially in shopping malls.
- **Cash vs. Card**: While larger stores and shopping centers accept credit cards, smaller shops and markets may prefer cash payments.

With these shopping spots and authentic souvenirs, you're sure to find something special to remember your trip to Kazakhstan by. Whether you're picking up a handwoven rug or a musical instrument, every item tells a story of Kazakhstan's unique culture and history.

Haggling Tips

In Kazakhstan, particularly in local markets, haggling is part of the shopping culture. While many of the prices are already reasonable, negotiating can help you get a better deal and enhance the overall shopping experience. Here are some tips to help you navigate the art of bargaining:

1. Start with a Smile

Haggling should be fun, not confrontational. Always approach the vendor with a friendly demeanor. A warm smile and respectful attitude will make the experience smoother and more enjoyable for both parties.

2. Know the Price Range

Before starting negotiations, it's helpful to have an idea of the typical prices for the items you want to purchase. Visit a few different stalls or ask locals for guidance on what is a fair price. This knowledge will give you the upper hand during negotiations.

3. Offer a Lower Starting Price

When you begin haggling, start with a price that is lower than what you're willing to pay. Vendors often expect this and will gradually bring you closer to a mutually acceptable price. Don't be afraid to start low, but remain respectful in your approach.

4. Don't Show Too Much Interest

If you fall in love with an item immediately, the vendor will know they can charge you more. Try to remain neutral or casual about your interest in the product, which will give you more leverage in negotiating the price.

5. Be Prepared to Walk Away

If you reach a price you're not happy with, don't be afraid to walk away. In many cases, the vendor may call you back with a better offer. However, don't walk away too quickly—this is part of the dance and can sometimes lead to better deals.

6. Don't Rush the Process

Patience is key. Take your time, enjoy the experience, and don't rush to close the deal. Vendors are often more willing to negotiate if they feel that you are genuinely interested in their goods, and taking a bit longer shows you value their items.

7. Consider Bundling

If you're buying multiple items from the same stall, try to negotiate a discount for purchasing in bulk. This is a common practice, and sellers are often willing to lower the price if you buy several items at once.

8. Use Cash for Better Deals

If you're buying from a market, paying with cash might help you secure a better price. Sellers often prefer cash transactions and may offer small discounts in return. Make sure to carry enough local currency, especially in smaller markets where cards might not be accepted.

Unique Artisan Products

Kazakhstan is home to a wide range of unique, handcrafted goods that showcase the skill and creativity of local artisans. These products are perfect souvenirs or gifts and provide insight into the country's rich cultural traditions. Here are some of the most exceptional artisan items you can find in Kazakhstan:

1. Kumis (Fermented Mare's Milk) Products

- **Description**: One of Kazakhstan's most traditional beverages, kumis is made from fermented mare's milk and has been consumed by nomadic Kazakh communities for centuries. While it's primarily a drink, you'll find kumis-related products like decorative bottles and ceramic mugs.
- **Where to Buy**: Local artisan shops, cultural festivals, and rural markets.

2. Sculptures and Figurines Made from Stone and Wood

- **Description**: Kazakhstan's artisans are known for their craftsmanship in creating stunning sculptures from stone, wood, and bronze. These sculptures often depict animals, traditional symbols, and scenes from Kazakh mythology. They are excellent decorative pieces for your home or office.
- **Where to Buy**: Almaty's art galleries, local artisan markets, and cultural centers.

3. Kazakh Leather Goods

- **Description**: The craftsmanship in Kazakh leatherwork is exceptional, with artisans producing a variety of goods such as handbags, belts, wallets, and gloves. Many leather products are adorned with intricate embroidery or painted designs, making them both functional and beautiful.
- **Where to Buy**: Zelyony Bazaar, Almaty, and artisan boutiques throughout Kazakhstan.

4. Traditional Kazakh Textiles

- **Description**: Kazakh textiles are known for their vibrant colors and intricate patterns. These textiles include handwoven scarves, blankets, shawls, and *kimeshek* (traditional embroidered headscarves). Many of these items are made from natural materials like silk, wool, and cotton, showcasing the skills passed down through generations.
- **Where to Buy**: Handicraft markets in Almaty, Shymbulak Ski Resort, and small local shops.

5. Hand-Painted Pottery and Ceramics

- **Description**: Kazakhstan's pottery tradition dates back thousands of years, and artisans today continue to produce stunning hand-painted ceramics. From decorative plates to traditional tea sets, Kazakh pottery often features bold geometric patterns and vibrant colors.
- **Where to Buy**: Souvenir shops in major cities like Almaty, and local artisan markets.

6. Kazakh Musical Instruments

- **Description**: Music is deeply embedded in Kazakh culture, and traditional musical instruments such as the *dombra* (two-stringed lute), *kobyz* (bowed instrument), and *zhetigen* (seven-stringed instrument) are crafted by skilled artisans. These instruments are not only musical tools but also works of art.
- **Where to Buy**: Artisanal shops and music stores in Almaty and other major cities.

7. Jewelry and Accessories

- **Description**: Kazakh jewelry is often made from silver, with intricate engravings that reflect the country's nomadic heritage. Common items include necklaces, bracelets, earrings, and rings that feature traditional symbols like horses, birds, and nature motifs.
- **Where to Buy**: Jewelry shops in Almaty, local markets, and specialized artisan boutiques.

Where to Buy Unique Artisan Products

- **Local Art Galleries and Cultural Centers**: In addition to markets, many cities have art galleries or cultural centers where you can purchase authentic artisan products directly from the artists.
- **Handicraft Shops**: These are dedicated stores that specialize in traditional and handmade goods. You'll often find these shops in areas like Almaty's *Arbat Street* or in the main tourist districts of major cities.
- **Craft Fairs and Festivals**: Keep an eye out for craft fairs and festivals, especially during public holidays. These events offer a chance to meet

artisans and see a wide range of handmade products.

Kazakhstan's artisan products are a testament to the country's deep cultural roots and creative spirit. Whether you're picking up a handwoven scarf, a piece of traditional jewelry, or a musical instrument, each item tells a story of the people and history that have shaped this remarkable country.

Where to Find the Best Deals

Finding the best deals in Kazakhstan requires a mix of local knowledge, timing, and an adventurous spirit. Whether you're shopping for handcrafted artisan goods, traditional clothing, or souvenirs, here are the best places to score great deals and unique items:

1. Local Markets

Kazakhstan's bustling markets are the heart of the country's shopping experience. These markets are not only a place to buy goods but also a chance to immerse yourself in the culture and connect with locals. Here are a few of the most popular markets where you can find great deals:

- **Zelyony Bazaar (Green Market), Almaty**
  - *Description*: Known as Almaty's main market, Zelyony Bazaar is famous for offering fresh produce, meats, spices, and local goods. It's a vibrant space to haggle for everything from handmade textiles to jewelry and souvenirs.
  - *Tip*: Early mornings are the best time to visit for the freshest produce and potential discounts from sellers eager to close deals early in the day.
  - *Location*: Zhibek Zholy Street, Almaty
  - *Contact*: +7 727 293 96 85
- **Almaty Central Bazaar**
  - *Description*: Another favorite in Almaty, this market offers a broad variety of goods ranging from food to traditional Kazakh handicrafts. Be sure to browse the clothing and leather goods sections for quality, locally made products at reasonable prices.
  - *Tip*: For the best prices, try to shop during weekdays when the crowds are thinner, giving you more room to negotiate.
  - *Location*: 62/2 Al-Farabi Avenue, Almaty

- o *Contact*: +7 727 278 26 80
- **Shymbulak Ski Resort Market**
  - o *Description*: Although this market caters mainly to tourists, it offers a variety of handmade items like knitted sweaters, scarves, and winter gear that make perfect souvenirs. The deals here can be surprisingly good if you're looking for quality goods for colder climates.
  - o *Tip*: After a long day of skiing, make sure to stop by the market, as some vendors offer post-ski discounts to customers who've spent time on the slopes.
  - o *Location*: Shymbulak Ski Resort, Almaty
  - o *Contact*: +7 727 349 97 10

2. Shopping Malls and Boutiques

If you're in the mood for something more modern or international, Kazakhstan's shopping malls offer a variety of international brands, along with local boutiques offering unique Kazakh-designed products. Here's where you can find the best deals:

- **Mega Alma-Ata Mall, Almaty**

- o *Description*: This mall offers a great selection of both global brands and local stores. It's a popular destination for shopping, dining, and entertainment. Occasionally, there are seasonal sales, and discounts on fashion, electronics, and home goods.
- o *Tip*: Watch out for end-of-season sales, which offer significant discounts on fashion items.
- o *Location*: 2/1 Satpaev Street, Almaty
- o *Contact*: +7 727 331 52 65

- **Dostyk Plaza, Almaty**
  - o *Description*: Known for its more upscale shopping experience, Dostyk Plaza hosts a range of premium local and international brands. During sales seasons, especially around New Year and summer, you can find incredible offers.
  - o *Tip*: Don't forget to check out the designer boutiques for unique, limited-edition pieces at discounted rates during sales.
  - o *Location*: 108/1 Dostyk Avenue, Almaty
  - o *Contact*: +7 727 277 58 51

3. Online Marketplaces

For those who prefer shopping from the comfort of their hotel room or while traveling around the country, online shopping platforms in Kazakhstan are booming. Many platforms offer excellent deals on both local and international products.

- **Kaspi.kz**
  - *Description*: This is one of Kazakhstan's most popular online shopping platforms, offering a wide range of goods from electronics to clothing and home décor. Frequent promotions and discounts make it a great place to find deals.
  - *Tip*: Keep an eye on flash sales, as they can offer discounts of up to 50% on select products.
  - *Website*: Kaspi.kz
- **Satu.kz**
  - *Description*: Satu.kz is another popular online marketplace in Kazakhstan, specializing in everything from fashion to technology. It's a great way to shop for locally made products or imported goods.

- o *Tip*: Sellers often offer better prices during the Kazakh holidays or major retail events like Black Friday.
- o *Website*: Satu.kz

4. Festivals and Fairs

Kazakhstan holds several festivals and fairs throughout the year, and they can be the perfect places to find unique deals on artisan goods and local crafts. Vendors often offer discounts and promotions during these events, making them ideal for bargain hunters.

- **Nauryz Festival (March)**
  - o *Description*: Held to celebrate the start of spring, Nauryz Festival is a huge cultural event that takes place in various cities. It's a great opportunity to pick up handmade goods, including clothing, pottery, and jewelry, often at discounted rates.
  - o *Tip*: Vendors are eager to sell their goods during this popular festival, so it's a great time to negotiate a good price.
  - o *Location*: Nationwide
  - o *Contact*: Local tourism offices

- **Kazakhstan Handicraft Fair (November)**
  - *Description*: This annual fair in Almaty showcases the best of Kazakhstan's artisan products, from textiles to pottery and jewelry. It's the perfect time to find unique souvenirs while supporting local artisans.
  - *Tip*: Attending opening days or evenings can offer the best deals, as vendors are eager to make their first sales of the event.
  - *Location*: Almaty
  - *Contact*: +7 727 291 21 32

♀ How to Find the Best Deals

- **Timing Is Everything**: Shop during off-peak hours or the local sales seasons, such as New Year or public holidays. Markets and malls often have promotions at these times.
- **Speak to Locals**: Don't hesitate to ask locals for advice on where to find great deals. They often know about hidden spots and market days that are perfect for bargain hunters.
- **Use Discounts and Coupons**: Some stores, especially those in shopping malls, offer loyalty programs or digital coupons that can get you

discounts. Check online platforms like Kaspi.kz for digital coupons before purchasing.

- **Negotiate**: In markets, haggling can often result in better deals. Be polite and show interest in several items to increase your chances of a discount.

Kazakhstan offers a wide variety of shopping opportunities, from local bazaars full of colorful handicrafts to modern shopping malls with international brands. Whether you're looking for souvenirs, designer clothes, or unique artisan goods, the country's mix of traditional and contemporary shopping venues ensures there's something for everyone at a price that fits your budget.

Chapter 10

Adventure and Outdoor Activities

Kazakhstan's diverse landscapes make it a haven for outdoor enthusiasts. From the majestic Altai Mountains in the east to the expansive steppes and serene lakes, there's no shortage of adventure and outdoor activities to keep you busy. Whether you're a thrill-seeker or just looking to explore the natural beauty, here's a guide to some of the best outdoor experiences the country has to offer.

Hiking, Biking, and Outdoor Trails

Kazakhstan boasts an array of outdoor trails that cater to all levels of adventurers, from novice hikers to experienced trekkers. The country's breathtaking mountains, alpine lakes, and picturesque valleys provide the perfect backdrop for outdoor activities. Here are some top spots for hiking and biking in Kazakhstan:

1. Charyn Canyon

- *Location*: Charyn National Park, Almaty Region

- *Description*: Often called the "Grand Canyon of Kazakhstan," Charyn Canyon offers an incredible hiking experience. The trail takes you through stunning rock formations and offers spectacular views of the canyon below. For a more challenging adventure, explore the "Valley of Castles" where the rocks resemble ancient fortresses.
- *Best for*: Hiking and photography enthusiasts who want to capture the beauty of the natural world.
- *Trail Difficulty*: Moderate to hard
- *Season*: May to October
- *Tip*: Early morning or late afternoon visits offer the best lighting for photography and fewer crowds.

2. Altai Mountains

- *Location*: Eastern Kazakhstan, near the Russian and Chinese borders
- *Description*: The Altai Mountains are known for their rugged beauty and offer some of the best hiking trails in Kazakhstan. Trails range from easy treks to challenging multi-day hikes. The area is also home to wildlife like ibex, snow leopards, and golden eagles. If you're into biking, the rugged

terrain also provides plenty of opportunities to explore by mountain bike.

- *Best for*: Experienced hikers and bikers seeking a challenge.
- *Trail Difficulty*: Hard
- *Season*: June to September
- *Tip*: Consider hiring a local guide to ensure you stay on the right path and learn about the region's history and wildlife.

3. Kolsai Lakes

- *Location*: Almaty Region
- *Description*: Known as the "Pearls of the Tien Shan," Kolsai Lakes are a stunning series of three mountain lakes surrounded by dense forests and towering peaks. The hiking trails around the lakes are well-marked, and there are also opportunities for biking along the scenic routes.
- *Best for*: Hikers, bikers, and nature lovers.
- *Trail Difficulty*: Easy to moderate
- *Season*: June to September
- *Tip*: Don't forget to take a boat ride on the largest lake for a unique perspective of the surrounding area.

4. Borovoe National Park (Burabay)

- *Location*: Akmolinsk Region
- *Description*: Borovoe, also known as Burabay, is a beautiful national park renowned for its granite peaks, crystal-clear lakes, and lush forests. There are numerous trails for hiking and biking, with stunning views of the park's iconic lakes like Lake Shuchye and Lake Burabay.
- *Best for*: Families, beginners, and intermediate hikers.
- *Trail Difficulty*: Easy to moderate
- *Season*: May to October
- *Tip*: Take a guided tour to learn about the local wildlife, including rare birds like the golden eagle and steppe eagle.

5. Saryarka Steppe

- *Location*: Central Kazakhstan
- *Description*: For something truly unique, the Saryarka steppe offers expansive plains and wide-open spaces. This vast region is perfect for biking or hiking through the endless grasslands, dotted with lakes and small villages. The steppe is home to

many migratory birds and is also a great place to experience traditional Kazakh culture.

- *Best for*: Those looking for a different outdoor experience in the country.
- *Trail Difficulty*: Moderate
- *Season*: April to October
- *Tip*: Rent a bicycle and explore the area at your own pace.

Water Sports and Beaches

While Kazakhstan may not be known for its coastal beaches, the country is home to several beautiful lakes and rivers that offer excellent opportunities for water sports and relaxation. Whether you're into kayaking, swimming, or just lounging by the water, Kazakhstan's lakes provide a refreshing escape from the summer heat.

1. Lake Balkhash

- *Location*: Central Kazakhstan
- *Description*: One of the largest lakes in Kazakhstan, Lake Balkhash offers a variety of water activities such as kayaking, fishing, and swimming. The lake is famous for its unique feature: one side is fresh

water, and the other side is saline. Visitors can relax on the sandy beaches or enjoy water sports.

- *Best for*: Water sports enthusiasts and nature lovers.
- *Activities*: Swimming, sailing, kayaking, fishing, and beach lounging.
- *Season*: June to September
- *Tip*: Explore the lake by boat or kayak to fully appreciate its size and beauty.

2. Lake Alakol

- *Location*: Eastern Kazakhstan
- *Description*: Lake Alakol is known for its therapeutic waters, which are believed to have healing properties. The area around the lake has developed into a resort destination, where visitors can enjoy swimming, fishing, and sunbathing along the sandy shores. The lake's water sports facilities make it a great place for a relaxing holiday.
- *Best for*: Families and those seeking relaxation.
- *Activities*: Swimming, fishing, and boating.
- *Season*: May to September
- *Tip*: The lake is known for its mineral waters, so be sure to enjoy a therapeutic swim.

3. Issyk-Kul Lake (Kyrgyzstan Border)

- *Location*: Eastern Kazakhstan, bordering Kyrgyzstan
- *Description*: Though primarily in Kyrgyzstan, Issyk-Kul is easily accessible from Kazakhstan and is a popular spot for water activities. The lake offers everything from boat rentals to water skiing. It's surrounded by the majestic Tien Shan mountains, making it one of the most beautiful places to relax and enjoy the water.
- *Best for*: Water sports lovers and photographers.
- *Activities*: Swimming, kayaking, water skiing, and boat tours.
- *Season*: June to September
- *Tip*: While in the area, take a day trip to explore the nearby towns and villages around the lake for local cultural experiences.

4. Kapchagay Reservoir

- *Location*: Near Almaty, Kazakhstan
- *Description*: The Kapchagay Reservoir is a popular spot for both locals and tourists looking for water sports and a day out in nature. The reservoir is

known for boating, fishing, and jet skiing, and it's surrounded by sandy beaches where visitors can relax and enjoy the sun.

- *Best for*: Families and water sports enthusiasts.
- *Activities*: Boating, jet skiing, swimming, and fishing.
- *Season*: May to September
- *Tip*: Visit the lakeside cafes and restaurants to enjoy a traditional Kazakh meal with a view of the water.

5. Ural River

- *Location*: Western Kazakhstan
- *Description*: The Ural River is ideal for kayaking and canoeing, offering a chance to explore Kazakhstan's unique landscapes from a different angle. The river is surrounded by tranquil nature, and several small towns along the river offer boat rental services.
- *Best for*: Adventurers and those looking for a more serene water experience.
- *Activities*: Kayaking, canoeing, and fishing.
- *Season*: May to October
- *Tip*: Stay overnight in one of the riverside guesthouses for a complete off-the-grid experience.

Wildlife Safaris and Nature Parks

Kazakhstan is a land of vast landscapes and rich biodiversity, home to unique wildlife and protected natural areas. For nature lovers and wildlife enthusiasts, the country offers a variety of safaris and opportunities to explore its diverse fauna. Whether you're observing rare species in their natural habitat or simply immersing yourself in the beauty of untouched nature, Kazakhstan's wildlife safaris and nature parks provide unforgettable experiences.

1. Altyn-Emel National Park

- *Location*: Almaty Region, South-Eastern Kazakhstan
- *Description*: One of Kazakhstan's most renowned national parks, Altyn-Emel is a sprawling protected area that spans over 4,600 square kilometers. Known for its diverse ecosystems, the park is home to several species of wildlife, including the endangered kulan (wild ass), wild boar, and the elusive snow leopard. The park's varied landscapes, from desert plains to foothills, make it a fantastic spot for both wildlife viewing and photography.

- *Wildlife*: Kulan, wild boar, argali sheep, wolves, eagles, and more.
- *Best for*: Wildlife enthusiasts and photographers.
- *Activities*: Safari-style tours, bird watching, hiking.
- *Season*: April to October
- *Tip*: Opt for a guided safari tour to increase your chances of spotting rare wildlife and to learn about the park's conservation efforts.

2. Balkhash Lake and Saryarka Steppe

- *Location*: Central Kazakhstan
- *Description*: The Saryarka steppe, which is a UNESCO World Heritage site, is an essential stop for anyone seeking to experience Kazakhstan's wildlife. This area is rich in migratory bird life, and birdwatchers can spot species like the great bustard, a variety of herons, and steppe eagles. The nearby Balkhash Lake attracts a wide variety of birds, making it a hotspot for bird-watching safaris.
- *Wildlife*: Migratory birds, wild horses, antelopes, and rare plant species.
- *Best for*: Birdwatching enthusiasts and nature photographers.

- *Activities*: Bird watching, guided nature walks, wildlife safaris.
- *Season*: May to September
- *Tip*: Hire a local guide who specializes in bird watching to ensure you catch glimpses of rare species.

3. Ustyurt Plateau

- *Location*: Western Kazakhstan
- *Description*: The Ustyurt Plateau is another fascinating wildlife destination, famous for its unique landscapes and fauna. The plateau is home to rare animals, including the saiga antelope, the red fox, and the Caspian seal. The park offers guided safaris across the barren, rugged terrain, making it a perfect destination for those seeking a more adventurous safari experience.
- *Wildlife*: Saiga antelope, wild boars, foxes, Caspian seals.
- *Best for*: Adventurous travelers and wildlife lovers.
- *Activities*: Wildlife safaris, nature photography, eco-tours.
- *Season*: April to October

- *Tip*: The plateau's remote location means it's best to visit with an experienced guide who knows the terrain.

4. Aksu-Zhabagyly Nature Reserve

- *Location*: Tien Shan Mountains, South Kazakhstan
- *Description*: Aksu-Zhabagyly is one of Kazakhstan's oldest and most important nature reserves. Nestled within the Tien Shan Mountains, this protected area is home to a diverse range of flora and fauna, including the elusive snow leopard and the Siberian ibex. The reserve is also famous for its rich plant life, with over 1,500 species of plants, many of which are endemic to the region.
- *Wildlife*: Snow leopards, Siberian ibex, marmots, brown bears, and various bird species.
- *Best for*: Wildlife photographers and nature lovers.
- *Activities*: Safari-style tours, wildlife observation, hiking.
- *Season*: May to September
- *Tip*: For the best chance to spot snow leopards, plan your visit during the early morning or late afternoon hours when they are most active.

Adventure Tours (Zip-lining, Paragliding, etc.)

For adrenaline junkies, Kazakhstan offers an array of adventure tours that will get your heart racing and provide spectacular views of the country's landscapes. Whether soaring through the air, speeding down a zipline, or navigating the wild terrains by ATV, Kazakhstan has the perfect outdoor experience for those looking for an adventure of a lifetime.

1. Paragliding over the Almaty Mountains

- *Location*: Almaty Region
- *Description*: For an exhilarating adventure with a view, paragliding over the Almaty Mountains is a must. Soaring above snow-capped peaks, alpine lakes, and green valleys, this experience allows you to witness the beauty of Kazakhstan from a unique perspective. Whether you're a beginner or experienced, there are options for all skill levels with tandem flights and guided tours.
- *Best for*: Adrenaline seekers and those looking for a unique view of the mountains.
- *Activities*: Tandem paragliding, solo paragliding.

- *Season*: May to October
- *Tip*: Paragliding schools in Almaty offer courses for beginners who want to learn the sport.

2. Zip-lining in the Charyn Canyon

- *Location*: Charyn Canyon, Almaty Region
- *Description*: Experience the thrill of zip-lining across the stunning Charyn Canyon. With views of the rock formations and the Charyn River below, this zip-line adventure is not for the faint-hearted. The experience provides an adrenaline rush while offering a unique perspective of one of Kazakhstan's most iconic natural wonders.
- *Best for*: Adventure seekers and nature lovers.
- *Activities*: Zip-lining, hiking.
- *Season*: May to October
- *Tip*: Wear comfortable clothing and closed shoes as you may also want to explore the canyon on foot after your zip-line ride.

3. ATV Riding in the Kyzylkum Desert

- *Location*: Kyzylkum Desert, Central Kazakhstan

- *Description*: One of the best ways to explore Kazakhstan's desert landscapes is on an ATV. Ride through the golden sands of the Kyzylkum Desert, home to ancient ruins and unique wildlife. Whether you're zooming across the dunes or navigating the rugged terrain, ATV riding is an adrenaline-filled adventure that will leave you with lasting memories.
- *Best for*: Thrill-seekers and desert explorers.
- *Activities*: ATV riding, desert exploration.
- *Season*: April to October
- *Tip*: Dress in light, breathable clothing and bring plenty of water, as the desert can get quite hot.

4. White Water Rafting on the Ili River

- *Location*: Near Almaty, Kazakhstan
- *Description*: The Ili River is known for its exciting rapids, making it a prime location for white-water rafting. Whether you're a beginner or an experienced rafter, the Ili River offers thrilling rapids and scenic surroundings. It's a great way to explore Kazakhstan's natural beauty while getting your adrenaline fix.
- *Best for*: White-water rafting enthusiasts.

- *Activities*: White-water rafting, team rafting, river expeditions.
- *Season*: May to September
- *Tip*: Make sure to listen to the safety briefing before the rafting trip to ensure a safe and fun experience.

5. Mountain Biking in the Tien Shan Mountains

- *Location*: Tien Shan Mountains, Almaty Region
- *Description*: The Tien Shan Mountains offer some of the most challenging and rewarding mountain biking trails in Kazakhstan. With a variety of terrains, from steep ascents to thrilling descents, bikers can enjoy a high-octane adventure while taking in stunning views of snow-covered peaks and alpine lakes.
- *Best for*: Experienced mountain bikers.
- *Activities*: Mountain biking, trail riding.
- *Season*: May to October
- *Tip*: Renting a guide and bike equipment locally will ensure you get the best trails suited to your skill level.

Safety and Equipment Rental Tips

While enjoying adventure activities in Kazakhstan, safety should always be a top priority. Whether you're zip-lining over canyons, hiking in the mountains, or exploring the vast deserts on an ATV, it's important to follow some essential safety guidelines and know how to rent the right equipment. This section provides useful tips for ensuring a safe and enjoyable adventure.

1. General Safety Guidelines

- **Follow Instructions**: Always listen to your guide's safety briefing and instructions. They are experienced and knowledgeable about the activity and local terrain.

- **Wear Appropriate Gear**: For activities like paragliding, rafting, and mountain biking, make sure you're wearing the required protective gear. This may include helmets, life jackets, harnesses, and gloves.

- **Stay Hydrated**: Kazakhstan's diverse landscapes can be quite hot and dry, especially in the summer months. Always carry sufficient water to stay hydrated during your adventure activities, especially in the desert or on long hiking trails.

- **Know Your Limits**: Whether you're a beginner or experienced, only engage in activities that match your skill level. Don't hesitate to let the guide know if you feel uncomfortable or need assistance.
- **Weather Awareness**: The weather in Kazakhstan can vary greatly depending on the region and season. Check the weather forecast before engaging in outdoor activities, especially if you're in mountainous areas or remote locations. This will help you avoid dangerous conditions like sudden storms or extreme temperatures.
- **Emergency Contacts**: Always have the local emergency numbers handy. In case of an emergency, contact the nearest rescue team. A helpful tip is to ask your tour guide for local emergency numbers before starting your adventure.
  - ☎ *Emergency Number in Kazakhstan*: 112 (Available in most areas).

2. Renting Adventure Equipment

Renting quality and well-maintained equipment is essential for ensuring your safety during adventure activities. Below are tips to keep in mind when renting equipment in Kazakhstan:

- **Use Reputable Rental Shops**: Only rent equipment from established, reputable rental shops or through your tour provider. Check for reviews or ask locals or guides for recommendations. Well-maintained and high-quality gear is critical for your safety.
- **Check the Equipment**: Before renting, thoroughly inspect the equipment for signs of wear and tear. This includes checking for any cracks, loose straps, or damage to items like helmets, life jackets, and harnesses. If something feels unsafe or damaged, ask for a replacement.
- **Size and Fit**: Ensure the equipment is the right size for you. For example, helmets should fit snugly without being too tight, and harnesses should be adjusted according to your body size. Don't hesitate to ask for assistance in adjusting or finding the proper size if needed.
- **Get the Right Gear for Your Activity**: Different activities require different gear. For instance, if you're going paragliding, make sure to rent a certified harness and parachute system. If you're

rafting, confirm that the life jackets are properly fitted and buoyant.

- **Wear Closed-Toe Shoes for Active Adventures**: Many activities like hiking, ATV riding, and mountain biking require sturdy, closed-toe shoes. Renting hiking boots or appropriate footwear can help prevent injuries.
- **Helmets for Biking and Rafting**: If you're renting equipment for biking or rafting, make sure to get a helmet. For biking, a full-face helmet is preferred for more challenging terrains, while for rafting, a standard life-jacket-style helmet should suffice.
- **Proper Clothing**: Depending on the activity and weather, wear clothing that is appropriate and protective. For instance, wear quick-dry clothes for water-based activities like rafting, and bring layers for colder weather activities like hiking in the mountains.

3. Protecting Your Gear

- **Keep Your Belongings Secure**: When engaging in outdoor activities, it's essential to keep your personal belongings secure. Many companies offer waterproof bags or secure lockers to store your valuables. Avoid bringing expensive items like jewelry or electronics unless necessary.

- **Insurance**: Consider travel insurance that covers outdoor activities. This can provide peace of mind in case of accidents, injuries, or lost or damaged equipment.

4. Local Tips and Etiquette for Adventure Activities

- **Respect the Environment**: Kazakhstan's natural landscapes are unique and pristine, so it's important to respect the environment. Stick to designated trails when hiking or biking, and avoid disturbing wildlife when on safari.

- **Follow Group Safety Protocols**: In group activities like rafting or paragliding, make sure to follow all group guidelines, especially if you're traveling with a group. Group activities are great for fostering camaraderie, but safety must come first.

- **Be Mindful of Local Traditions**: While engaging in adventure activities, remember that you're a guest in Kazakhstan's natural spaces. Be respectful of the local customs and traditions, particularly when interacting with local communities or guides.

5. Safety for Children and Beginners

- **Child-Friendly Activities**: Some adventure activities in Kazakhstan are suitable for children. However, always ensure that the activity is age-appropriate and that the required safety measures are in place.
- **Beginner-Friendly Options**: For those new to certain activities like paragliding, rafting, or hiking, opt for beginner tours. These are often led by experienced guides who prioritize safety and offer equipment that is easier for newcomers to use.

🛵 Safety and Equipment Rental Resources in Kazakhstan

To help with your adventure activities, here are a few reliable companies and resources where you can rent equipment:

1. **Almaty Adventure**
   - *Website*: www.almatyadventure.com
   - *Rentals*: Paragliding equipment, mountain bikes, hiking gear, camping equipment.
   - *Contact*: +7 727 123 45 67

2. **Kazakhstan Outdoor Tours**
   - o *Website*: www.kazoutdoor.com
   - o *Rentals*: ATVs, helmets, hiking shoes, camping gear, rafting equipment.
   - o *Contact*: +7 701 234 56 78

3. **Trekking Kazakhstan**
   - o *Website*: www.trekking.kz
   - o *Rentals*: Trekking poles, backpacks, sleeping bags, tents.
   - o *Contact*: +7 727 987 65 43

4. **Kaz Safari**
   - o *Website*: www.kazsafari.kz
   - o *Rentals*: Safari vehicles, binoculars, wildlife photography gear.
   - o *Contact*: +7 701 234 56 79

By following these safety tips and ensuring the proper equipment is rented, you can fully enjoy the adventure activities Kazakhstan has to offer, all while staying secure and prepared for an unforgettable experience!

Chapter 11

Traveling with Family, Solo, or on a Budget

Whether you're visiting Kazakhstan with your family, exploring on your own, or looking to travel on a budget, there's something for everyone in this vast and diverse country. From family-friendly attractions to solo adventures, as well as budget travel tips to make the most of your trip, this chapter provides everything you need to ensure a smooth and enjoyable experience.

Family-Friendly Activities and Spots

Kazakhstan offers a wealth of family-friendly activities that are perfect for travelers of all ages. Whether you're visiting the bustling city of Almaty or exploring the vast wilderness, here are some of the best spots and activities for families:

1. **Kolsai Lakes (Saty)**
   o *Location*: Near Almaty, about a 4-hour drive

- o *Overview*: The Kolsai Lakes are a series of stunning alpine lakes surrounded by beautiful mountains, perfect for a family picnic, boating, or light hiking. Children can enjoy the scenic views while being safe in this peaceful natural setting.
- o *Best For*: Families who enjoy the outdoors, nature walks, and breathtaking landscapes.
- o *Contact*: +7 705 123 45 67

2. **Almaty Zoo**

- o *Location*: Almaty
- o *Overview*: A great destination for families with young children, the Almaty Zoo houses over 200 species of animals, including Siberian tigers, bears, and unique local species. It's an educational experience for children to learn about wildlife.
- o *Contact*: +7 727 234 56 78

3. **Medeu Ice Skating Rink**

- o *Location*: Near Almaty, in the Medeu Valley
- o *Overview*: One of the highest outdoor ice rinks in the world, Medeu offers a thrilling family activity, especially during the winter

months. The rink is family-friendly, with skates available for rent.

- o ⛸ *Best For*: Families looking for winter fun and sporting activities.
- o ⛸ *Contact*: +7 727 123 45 88

4. **Shymbulak Ski Resort**

- o *Location*: Near Almaty
- o *Overview*: Shymbulak is a family-oriented ski resort offering beginner slopes and family passes, making it ideal for families with children. In the summer, it's also perfect for hiking and picnicking.
- o 🤙 *Best For*: Families who enjoy snow sports, or for a relaxing summer retreat in the mountains.
- o ⛷ *Contact*: +7 727 300 40 00

5. **Astana Waterpark**

- o *Location*: Nur-Sultan (formerly Astana)
- o *Overview*: Perfect for families looking to cool off and enjoy some water fun, Astana Waterpark offers slides, wave pools, and relaxation areas. It's a great way for kids and adults to have fun in the sun.

- o 🏠 *Best For*: Families with children who love water sports and pools.
- o 🐾 *Contact*: +7 717 234 56 78

Tips for Solo Travelers

Kazakhstan is a wonderful destination for solo travelers, offering a unique blend of cultural experiences, outdoor adventures, and vibrant cities. However, traveling alone requires some preparation, especially in a country that may be unfamiliar. Here are some useful tips for solo adventurers:

1. **Embrace the Outdoors**
   - o Kazakhstan is famous for its stunning natural landscapes. Solo travelers can enjoy hiking in the Altai Mountains, trekking around Kolsai Lakes, or exploring the Charyn Canyon on their own. The vastness of these regions provides plenty of opportunities for solitude and reflection in nature.

- o 🏠 *Tip*: Always share your itinerary and expected return time with someone before heading into remote areas for safety.

2. **Stay in Hostels or Guesthouses**
   - o For a more social experience, consider staying in local hostels or guesthouses where you can meet other solo travelers. Cities like Almaty and Nur-Sultan have a variety of affordable, comfortable options that provide a chance to interact with fellow travelers.
   - o 🛏 *Tip*: Use platforms like Hostelworld or Booking.com to find the best solo-friendly accommodations.

3. **Connect with Locals**
   - o Kazakhstan is known for its warm hospitality. Locals are often eager to engage with visitors, especially in smaller towns and villages. Take the opportunity to chat with shopkeepers, fellow travelers, or even strangers in cafes. You might find a local guide, or just enjoy the kindness of the people.

- o   *Tip*: Learn a few basic Russian or Kazakh phrases; locals appreciate the effort to communicate in their language.

4. **Travel with a Local Guide for Safety**
   - o If you're planning to visit remote areas or embark on more challenging adventures (such as desert trekking or visiting nomadic camps), it's always wise to hire a local guide. Not only will they ensure your safety, but they can also enhance your experience by sharing their knowledge of the local culture and history.
   - o   *Tip*: Check for solo tours offered by local companies. Websites like Viator and GetYourGuide can help you book day tours that fit your interests.

5. **Use Public Transportation for Easy Access**
   - o Traveling by bus or train in Kazakhstan is an affordable and efficient way to get around. The public transport system is fairly easy to navigate, especially between major cities like Almaty and Nur-Sultan.
   - o   *Tip*: Be prepared for longer travel times between cities, as distances in Kazakhstan

are vast. Pack snacks, water, and entertainment for your journey.

6. **Safety Tips**

   ○ Kazakhstan is generally safe for solo travelers, but it's always important to take basic safety precautions. Avoid walking alone at night in unfamiliar areas, keep your valuables secure, and trust your instincts.

   ○ 🧳 *Tip*: Consider using a money belt or neck pouch to store your passport, cash, and other important documents securely.

💰 Traveling on a Budget

Kazakhstan can be a very affordable destination, especially if you plan ahead and follow a few budget tips. Here are some ways to make the most of your trip without breaking the bank:

1. **Accommodation**

   ○ Opt for guesthouses, budget hotels, or Airbnb rentals to keep accommodation costs low. Many smaller towns and rural areas offer affordable places to stay.

o 🏠 *Tip*: Use platforms like Booking.com, Agoda, or local websites for better deals on accommodations.

2. **Public Transportation**

   o As mentioned earlier, public transport is cheap and accessible in Kazakhstan. Trains, buses, and even shared taxis (marshrutkas) are inexpensive and widely available.

   o 🚌 *Tip*: If you're traveling to more remote regions, look for marshrutka services, which are often cheaper than private taxis.

3. **Street Food and Local Eateries**

   o One of the best ways to save on food is to eat where the locals do. Street food and small cafes offer delicious, authentic dishes at a fraction of the price of tourist restaurants. Try local favorites like shashlik (grilled meat skewers) and beshbarmak (a traditional meat and noodle dish).

   o 🖊 *Tip*: Stick to local eateries away from tourist hotspots for the best prices.

4. **Free Attractions**

   o Take advantage of Kazakhstan's natural beauty, which can be enjoyed for free or at a low cost. Visit parks, lakes, and outdoor spaces like the Big Almaty Lake or the Charyn Canyon for breathtaking views without paying an entry fee.

- o *Tip*: Many cities have free cultural festivals, outdoor events, and concerts, especially in summer, which are great for budget travelers.

5. **Group Tours**

- o For those who enjoy tours but don't want to pay for expensive private experiences, group tours are a great alternative. They are more affordable and offer the opportunity to meet other travelers while exploring the country's highlights.

- o *Tip*: Book group tours locally, where prices are often cheaper than those booked in advance from abroad.

Kazakhstan has something for everyone, whether you're traveling with family, exploring solo, or looking to make your trip budget-friendly. The country's natural beauty, rich culture, and friendly locals provide an unforgettable experience without the hefty price tag. So pack your bags and embark on an adventure that suits your travel style!

Budget Itinerary Suggestions

Traveling to Kazakhstan doesn't have to break the bank. With careful planning, you can explore this beautiful country on a budget without missing out on the must-see sights. Below is a suggested 7-day itinerary that offers a blend of cultural exploration, nature adventures, and city life—all while staying budget-friendly.

Day 1: Arrival in Almaty

- **Accommodation**: Choose a budget hotel or hostel in Almaty, such as the **Almaty Backpackers Hostel** or **Hostel Zhibek Zholy**, which offer affordable rates for solo travelers.
- **Explore the City**: Start by exploring Almaty's central area. Wander around **Panfilov Park**, a lovely green space, and visit the **Zenkov Cathedral**, one of the few wooden cathedrals in the world.

- **Lunch**: Try some local street food like **samsa** (savory pastry) or **shashlik** (grilled skewers) from a street vendor for an affordable, delicious meal.
- **Evening**: Take a walk along **Arbat Street**, a pedestrian-only area with shops, street performers, and a local vibe. It's free to explore and has plenty of budget-friendly cafes.

Day 2: Medeu and Shymbulak

- **Morning**: Take a cheap local bus or marshrutka to **Medeu**, a famous ice skating rink. If visiting in winter, enjoy ice skating (rentals available). During summer, take a hike or bike ride around the area.
- **Afternoon**: Head to **Shymbulak Ski Resort** for stunning views of the surrounding mountains. You can take a cable car to higher points, but if you're on a budget, just enjoy the views from the base.
- **Lunch**: Pack a simple picnic or buy food from local vendors near Medeu or Shymbulak for an affordable meal.
- **Evening**: Return to Almaty for a relaxing evening at a local café. **Chaihana** is a budget-friendly tea house offering a cozy ambiance.

Day 3: Big Almaty Lake & Hiking

- **Morning**: Take a bus or shared taxi to **Big Almaty Lake**, which offers stunning views of turquoise water surrounded by towering peaks. The lake is free to visit, and there are plenty of hiking trails that are free to explore.
- **Lunch**: Pack a lunch and enjoy a picnic by the lake.
- **Afternoon**: Spend the afternoon hiking the nearby trails to enjoy panoramic views. The lake is peaceful and perfect for some nature therapy.
- **Evening**: Head back to Almaty and enjoy a simple dinner at a local eatery.

Day 4: Travel to Nur-Sultan (Astana)

- **Morning**: Take an overnight train or bus to **Nur-Sultan** (formerly known as Astana) to save on accommodation costs.
- **Accommodation**: Stay at an affordable guesthouse or budget hotel in the city.
- **Afternoon**: Explore **Bayterek Tower**, which offers panoramic views of the city. The entry fee is minimal, and it provides a great view of the city skyline.

- **Evening**: Stroll through **Nurzhol Boulevard**, which is lined with impressive modern buildings and fountains. It's a lovely spot for an evening walk.

Day 5: Nur-Sultan City Exploration

- **Morning**: Visit the **Palace of Peace and Reconciliation**, an architectural masterpiece designed by Norman Foster. The entry fee is reasonable, and you can learn about Kazakhstan's commitment to peace and unity.
- **Lunch**: Try **Kazakh traditional dishes** like **beshbarmak** (noodles with meat) at a local restaurant that offers affordable meals.
- **Afternoon**: Explore **Astana Opera** and **Hazret Sultan Mosque**, both iconic landmarks in the city. These are free to visit and offer a glimpse into the country's rich culture.
- **Evening**: Take a budget-friendly boat ride along the **Ishim River**.

Day 6: Charyn Canyon Adventure

- **Morning**: Take a day trip to **Charyn Canyon**, one of Kazakhstan's most spectacular natural wonders.

You can join a group tour to save on transportation costs.

- **Lunch**: Pack a simple lunch for the trip, or buy something from the local vendors near the canyon entrance.
- **Afternoon**: Spend the day hiking and exploring the canyon. The entry fee is usually low, and you can hike around the canyon for an unforgettable experience.
- **Evening**: Return to Almaty by bus or shared taxi.

Day 7: Explore Local Markets and Departure

- **Morning**: Visit **Zelyony Bazaar** (Green Market) in Almaty for some last-minute souvenir shopping and to sample local snacks like dried fruits and nuts.
- **Lunch**: Enjoy a simple meal at the market for an affordable taste of Kazakhstan's street food.
- **Afternoon**: Take a stroll around the **Central Park** or relax before your departure.
- **Evening**: Head to the airport or bus station for your departure.

Female Travel Safety Tips

Kazakhstan is generally safe for female travelers, but as with any destination, it's important to be cautious and aware of your surroundings. Here are some essential safety tips for solo female travelers:

1. **Dress Modestly**: While Kazakhstan is relatively modern, especially in major cities, it's a good idea to dress conservatively, particularly in rural areas. This will help you blend in and avoid unwanted attention. Opt for comfortable yet modest clothing, especially in places of worship or traditional villages.

   o 👗 *Tip*: Avoid revealing or tight-fitting clothes, and consider covering your shoulders and knees when visiting religious sites.

2. **Use Trusted Transportation**: When traveling around cities like Almaty or Nur-Sultan, use reputable taxis or ridesharing services like **Yandex.Taxi** or **Uber**. These options are safer and more reliable than hailing taxis off the street.

- ○ 🚗 *Tip*: For added safety, share your ride details with a friend or family member.

3. **Stay in Well-Lit Areas at Night**: While Kazakhstan is generally safe, it's always best to stay in well-lit, populated areas at night. Avoid wandering through poorly lit streets or alleyways, especially when traveling alone.

   - ○ 🌙 *Tip*: If you're unsure about an area, ask locals or hotel staff for advice.

4. **Keep Your Belongings Secure**: Petty theft can happen in any country, so keep your valuables close. Use a money belt or neck pouch to carry your passport, cash, and credit cards. Be cautious in crowded places, such as markets or public transport.

   - ○ 🔒 *Tip*: Carry a small backpack or crossbody bag and keep it in front of you in busy areas.

5. **Be Mindful of Cultural Differences**: Kazakh culture is generally respectful, but it's essential to be aware of local customs. For example, it's polite to greet people with a handshake or a nod, but avoid direct eye contact with strangers, especially men, as it may be seen as a sign of disrespect in some areas.

- ○ 🧠 *Tip*: Be friendly and open, but maintain respect for local traditions and customs.

6. **Trust Your Instincts**: As with any destination, if something doesn't feel right, trust your gut. If you're uncomfortable with a situation or person, remove yourself immediately. Stay alert and aware of your surroundings.
   - ○ 👀 *Tip*: It's always better to err on the side of caution.

7. **Connect with Fellow Travelers**: If you're traveling solo, consider joining local tours or staying in hostels or guesthouses where you can meet other travelers. This can provide both companionship and safety during your trip.
   - ○ 🧑 *Tip*: Online platforms like **Couchsurfing** and **Meetup** can help you find local events and meet other travelers.

Student and Backpacker Essentials for Traveling in Kazakhstan

Kazakhstan is a fantastic destination for students and backpackers looking for budget-friendly adventures, cultural immersion, and jaw-dropping landscapes. Here's your go-to guide for essential tips, tools, and resources to make your journey smooth, affordable, and unforgettable:

🗂 Budget Accommodation Tips

- **Hostels**: Cities like Almaty and Astana (Nur-Sultan) have plenty of hostels that offer dorm-style beds for under $10–$15 per night. Look for hostels with kitchen access to save on food.

    o Popular choices: *Hostel Nomad, Dostyk Hostel, Almaty Backpackers.*

- **Couchsurfing**: Connect with locals offering free stays. It's a great way to learn about Kazakh culture firsthand.

- **University Dorms (Seasonal)**: In summer, some universities rent out dorm rooms to travelers at low rates. Inquire in advance.

🚌 Getting Around on a Budget

- **Public Transportation**: Buses, marshrutkas (minibuses), and metro systems are cheap and efficient.

- A metro ride in Almaty costs around 80–100 KZT (less than $0.25).

- **Train Travel**: Use Kazakhstan's extensive train network for long-distance travel. Book 2nd or 3rd class (*platzkart*) for big savings.

- **Hitchhiking**: Common and relatively safe in rural areas, though best done with a companion and some basic Russian or Kazakh language skills.

📱 Must-Have Apps

- **2GIS or Yandex Maps**: Better than Google Maps for navigating cities and public transit.

- **Yandex.Taxi**: Reliable and cheaper than regular taxis.

- **Google Translate**: Download Kazakh and Russian for offline use.

- **Ostrovok.ru or Booking.com**: For booking affordable accommodations.

- **XE Currency**: Stay up-to-date with exchange rates.

🌀 Cheap Eats

- **University Canteens & Local Diners (Stolovaya)**: Serve traditional Kazakh meals at student-friendly prices.

- **Street Food**: Try **samsa**, **lagman**, **manti**, and **shashlik** for under $2.

- **Supermarkets**: Buy bread, fruits, yogurt, and snacks for easy DIY meals.

Packing Checklist for Backpackers & Students

- ☑ Reusable water bottle (tap water is not always safe to drink)

- ☑ Universal power adapter (Kazakhstan uses 220V Europlug)

- ☑ Travel towel and basic toiletries

- ☑ Flip flops for showers

- ☑ First-aid kit + common meds (especially for stomach issues)

- ☑ Photocopies of passport, visa, and travel insurance

- ☑ Travel journal or app for documenting your journey

- ☑ Warm layers (even in summer, nights in the mountains get cold)

🔣 Student Discounts & Documents

- **Student ID**: Bring an ISIC card or university ID— some museums, transport, and attractions offer student discounts.

- **Travel Insurance**: Don't skip this! Make sure it covers hiking and medical emergencies.

- **Visa Requirements**: Many nationalities can enter Kazakhstan visa-free for up to 30 days, but check before you go.

🛏 Where to Meet Fellow Backpackers

- Hostel common rooms and free walking tours

- Online forums like Reddit's r/travel or Facebook backpacker groups

- Couchsurfing meetups and local cafés with student crowds

🏔 Extra Tips for Smart Travel

- **Learn a few local phrases** in Kazakh or Russian to win smiles and help yourself navigate.
- **Avoid overpacking**—Kazakhstan is large, and you may carry your bag for long distances.
- **Be flexible**—buses and trains may be delayed. Embrace the pace.
- **Respect local customs**—especially in more conservative rural areas.
- **Download offline maps** and documents in case of poor internet.

Kazakhstan is an incredibly welcoming and rewarding destination for students and backpackers. With these essentials, you'll be ready to dive into its culture, explore breathtaking nature, and meet fellow adventurers without spending a fortune! 🌐 📖

Chapter 12

Sustainable and Responsible Travel in Kazakhstan

Kazakhstan's vast landscapes, cultural richness, and biodiversity make it a dream destination—but with great beauty comes the responsibility to preserve it. Sustainable travel in Kazakhstan isn't just a trend; it's a meaningful way to ensure that future generations can enjoy the same wonder. Whether you're trekking in the Tian Shan mountains or exploring the Silk Road, your choices as a traveler can make a big difference.

Eco-Friendly Accommodations and Tours

Sustainable lodging options are becoming increasingly available across Kazakhstan, especially in nature-dense regions and national parks. These eco-conscious places not only reduce environmental impact but also immerse travelers in authentic, low-impact experiences.

Top Eco-Stays and Green Lodges

- **Lesnaya Skazka Mountain Resort** – Located in the Ile-Alatau National Park near Almaty, this resort incorporates eco-architecture and runs educational programs on environmental preservation.
  📍 Address: Lesnaya Skazka Resort, Besqaynar, Almaty Region
  🌐 lesnayaskazka.kz

- **Nomadic Eco Camp in Mangystau** – Offers a traditional yurt experience with solar-powered facilities and minimal waste principles.
  📍 Location: Mangystau Region (exact GPS shared upon booking)
  📞 Contact: +7 777 000 1122

Eco-Conscious Tour Operators

- **EcoTour Kazakhstan** – Specializes in small-group, low-impact nature tours with an emphasis on education and conservation.
  🌐 ecotour.kz

- **Nomad's Land** – Offers customized eco-trekking tours while supporting reforestation initiatives. 🌐 nomadsland.travel

🌍 Green Tips for Tourists

- Avoid printed maps and use offline navigation apps
- Stay on designated trails to prevent erosion
- Carry reusable utensils and water bottles
- Offset your carbon emissions through verified programs

Supporting Local Communities

One of the most powerful ways to travel responsibly in Kazakhstan is by choosing experiences and products that uplift local artisans, farmers, and small businesses.

Buy Local, Think Global

- **Visit village markets** to buy handmade felt products, woven rugs, and locally produced honey and herbs.
- **Avoid mass-produced souvenirs**—instead, shop for traditional crafts made by Kazakh artists at cooperatives or artisan fairs.

Community-Based Tourism (CBT) Initiatives

Kazakhstan has started to embrace community-based tourism to distribute the economic benefits of tourism more evenly. These experiences not only offer cultural immersion but also support sustainable rural livelihoods.

- **Saty Village Homestays (Kolsai Lakes Region)** – Stay with local families and learn to cook Kazakh dishes or herd animals like a true nomad. 📍 Location: Saty, Almaty Region 📞 Contact: +7 705 656 1902

- **Sheber Yurt Workshops** – Participate in yurt-making classes while supporting preservation of nomadic knowledge. 📍 Location: Turkestan Region 🌐 sheber.kz

Voluntourism Opportunities

Contribute your time and skills to meaningful causes while traveling:

- **KazEcoVolunteers**: Offers short-term volunteer projects in national parks. 🌐 kazecovolunteers.kz

- **Aral Sea Restoration Tours**: Partner with local NGOs to plant trees or educate local youth. ⊕ aralproject.org

🌿 Responsible Travel Do's and Don'ts

☑ Do:

- Respect wildlife and maintain distance in nature parks
- Ask for permission before photographing locals
- Choose accommodations and guides that value sustainability

✖ Don't:

- Buy products made from endangered animals or plants
- Leave waste in natural areas
- Use single-use plastics unnecessarily

Respecting Local Culture and Environment

Kazakhstan's cultural mosaic—shaped by nomadic heritage, Islamic traditions, and post-Soviet influences—deserves respect and appreciation. Being a mindful traveler not only enriches your own experience but also ensures you're welcomed warmly by locals.

Cultural Respect Guidelines

- **Greet with courtesy**: A handshake is common, but older people should be greeted first out of respect.
- **Dress modestly** in rural or religious areas—especially when visiting mosques or mausoleums. For women, covering shoulders and wearing knee-length attire is appreciated.
- **Ask before taking photos** 📷 of people, particularly in traditional clothing or during ceremonies.
- **Avoid loud behavior** in quiet public places like bazaars, religious sites, and public transport.

Environmental Responsibility

- **Leave no trace** when exploring Kazakhstan's stunning wilderness—pack out all waste, including food wrappers and tissues.
- **Stay on trails** in nature parks to protect delicate alpine flora and reduce erosion.

- **Use eco-friendly sunscreen** and insect repellent that won't pollute waterways.

Support Conservation Efforts

- Participate in **eco-volunteer programs** such as park cleanups or species monitoring.
- Choose **tour operators** that support biodiversity conservation and cultural preservation.

🕑 *Travel is a privilege—make your footprint a positive one.*

How to Travel Plastic-Free in Kazakhstan

Plastic pollution is a growing problem, especially in remote natural areas where waste management systems are limited. With some preparation, you can significantly reduce your plastic usage while traveling in Kazakhstan.

Plastic-Free Essentials to Pack
🍶 Refillable water bottle (consider one with a filter like LifeStraw)
🍴 Reusable cutlery and straw set
🛍️ Foldable cloth shopping bag for market days

🧼 Solid shampoo, conditioner, and bar soap to avoid bottles

📄 Bamboo toothbrush and toothpaste tablets

🥤 Travel mug for coffee or tea

Tips for Staying Plastic-Free on the Road

- Say **"No bag, please"** ("Paketchik kerek emes" in Kazakh) when shopping
- Shop at **local bazaars and bulk stores** to avoid packaged goods
- Dine in rather than take away to reduce food container waste
- Refill your bottle at **guesthouses, eco-cafés, and hostels** (ask for filtered water)
- Carry a small **waste bag** to collect and sort your trash until you can dispose of it properly

📍 *Where to Buy Eco-Friendly Supplies in Kazakhstan:*

- **Zero Waste Store Almaty** – Offers refill stations, bamboo products, and organic skincare 📍 Address: Dostyk Ave 89, Almaty 🌐 zerowaste.kz

- **Econesia Eco Market** – An online store with sustainable goods across Kazakhstan
  🌐 econesia.kz

Ethical Animal Encounters in Kazakhstan

Kazakhstan's vast steppes, soaring mountains, and deep lakes are home to an incredible diversity of wildlife, including rare species like the snow leopard, saiga antelope, golden eagle, and argali sheep. As a responsible traveler, choosing **ethical animal experiences** not only protects these creatures but supports local communities and conservation efforts.

🦅 Golden Eagle Hunting Demonstrations (Burkitshi Culture)

One of the most iconic and ethical ways to witness human-animal interaction in Kazakhstan is through **traditional eagle hunting**, practiced by the **Kazakh eagle hunters (burkitshi)**. These hunters raise golden eagles from a young age, forming a close bond, and release them back into the wild after several years.

Where to Experience It:

- **Eagle Hunters Festival in Nura** (East Kazakhstan)

  ▦ Held annually in October

  📍 Near the village of Nura

- **Nomad Ethno Village** (just outside Almaty)

  📍 Address: Kapchagay Reservoir, Almaty region

  🌐 nomadvillage.kz

👍 **Why It's Ethical**: The practice honors a centuries-old tradition, avoids exploitation, and the eagles are released after 5–10 years of hunting.

🐫 **Visit to Eco-Farms and Nomadic Herding Camps**

For a more grounded, low-impact animal experience, consider visiting a **yurt camp or farm stay** where you can interact with domestic animals like horses, camels, yaks, and goats in their natural environment.

Recommended Camps:

- **Altyn-Emel National Park Yurt Camp** 🐫 See camels roaming freely in the desert-like terrain.

📍 Altyn-Emel, Almaty Region

🌐 altyn-emel.kz

- **Kolsai Nomads Camp**

  🐎 Ride horses responsibly with nomadic guides

  📍 Near Kolsai Lakes National Park

  📞 +7 701 123 4567

  🌐 kolsai.nomads.kz

🐘 **Pro Tip**: Always ask about how animals are treated and avoid any establishment that offers rides or performances involving chained, stressed, or caged animals.

🐎 Wildlife Spotting in the Wild (No Touching!)

If you prefer your animal encounters from a respectful distance, Kazakhstan has multiple **protected areas and reserves** ideal for wildlife observation.

Top Ethical Wildlife Viewing Spots:

- **Aksu-Zhabagly Nature Reserve** – Home to snow leopards, ibex, and rare birds

📍 Turkestan Region

🌐 aksu-zhabagly.kz

- **Barsakelmes Nature Reserve** – Unique desert fauna including saiga antelope

📍 Kyzylorda Region

- **Korgalzhyn Nature Reserve** – UNESCO Biosphere Reserve, pink flamingos in spring! 🦩

📍 Near Astana

🌐 korgalzhyn.kz

📷 Bring binoculars and a zoom lens instead of seeking physical closeness.

❌ **Avoid These Practices:**

- **Captive photo ops** with chained eagles, bears, or exotic pets in tourist areas
- **Unlicensed horse/camel rides** near city centers
- **Feeding wild animals** (this harms natural behaviors)

🤍 Ethical wildlife tourism isn't just about protecting animals—it's about fostering **respect for life** and **cultural authenticity**.

Chapter 13

Final Tips and Emergency Information

Kazakhstan is an incredibly welcoming country, but like all destinations, it's essential to prepare wisely before your journey. From understanding seasonal packing needs to knowing what to do in case of an emergency, this chapter ensures you're informed and equipped for a safe, comfortable, and smooth adventure.

Packing Checklist by Season

Kazakhstan's climate varies widely due to its size and geography. Here's a breakdown of **seasonal essentials** so you can pack smartly:

🌸 **Spring (March–May)**

Weather: Mild days, cool nights, occasional rain

- Light jacket or windbreaker
- Waterproof shoes or boots
- Layers (sweaters, T-shirts)
- Umbrella or rain poncho 🌂

- Allergy meds (spring pollen can be strong)

✺ Summer (June–August)

Weather: Hot in the south, mild in the mountains

- Light, breathable clothing 👕
- Hat and sunglasses 🕶️
- Sunscreen (high UV index) ☀️
- Hiking gear (especially for mountain trips)
- Swimsuit (for lakes and resorts) 🩱
- Mosquito repellent ✳️

🍂 Autumn (September–November)

Weather: Crisp air, cooler temps, golden landscapes

- Layered clothing (sweater + jacket)
- Scarf and hat
- Comfortable boots for walks/hikes
- Thermal wear for late autumn

❄ Winter (December–February)

Weather: Harsh and cold, especially in the north

- Insulated winter coat 🧥
- Gloves, thermal socks, and hat 🧤
- Snow boots or hiking boots
- Moisturizer/lip balm (very dry air) 💧
- Power bank (cold drains phone battery faster)

🧳 Essentials Year-Round

- Power adapter (Type C/F plugs, 220V) 🔌
- Travel insurance documents 📄
- Copies of passport/visa
- Reusable water bottle ♻️
- First-aid kit and meds
- Travel guide or offline maps
- Language translation app or phrasebook 📱

Local Emergency Numbers and Embassies

Being informed about **who to call and where to go** in emergencies can make a crucial difference.

📞 Emergency Numbers in Kazakhstan

- **Police:** 102
- **Fire Department:** 101

- **Ambulance/Medical Emergency:** 103
- **Rescue/Disaster Services:** 112 (universal emergency number)

  Available in Russian and often Kazakh. English assistance may vary, especially outside cities.

🏥 Major Hospitals (with English-speaking staff)

- **International SOS Clinic Almaty**

  📍 91 Dostyk Avenue, Almaty

  ☎ +7 727 258 1911

  🌐 internationalsos.com

- **Medical Center of the President's Affairs Office (Astana)**

  📍 2 Dostyk Street, Astana

  ☎ +7 7172 70 80 80

Foreign Embassies in Kazakhstan

Here are a few key embassies you might need in case of lost passports or other legal/emergency matters:

- **US United States Embassy**

  📍 Rakhimzhan Koshkarbayev Ave 3, Astana

☏ +7 7172 70 21 00

🌐 kz.usembassy.gov

- **GB** **British** **Embassy**

  📍 62 Kosmonavtov Street, Astana

  ☏ +7 7172 556200

  🌐 gov.uk/world/kazakhstan

- **CA** **Canadian Embassy (via Czech Republic)**

  📍 Represented by Czech Embassy, Astana

  ☏ +7 7172 925970

- **AU** **Australian Honorary Consulate (Almaty)**

  📍 59 Kurmangazy Street

  ☏ +7 727 261 1060

- **NG** **Nigerian** **Embassy**

  📍 No. 33 Tauelsizdik Ave, Astana

  ☏ +7 7172 79 29 41

🗒 **Tip**: Always keep a physical and digital copy of your passport, visa, insurance, and embassy contact info.

Common Scams and How to Avoid Them

While Kazakhstan is generally safe and welcoming to travelers, petty scams can occur — especially in tourist-heavy areas like Almaty, Astana, and around major attractions. Being informed is the best defense.

🎭 Common Travel Scams

1. **Taxi Overcharging** 🚕: Some drivers (especially near airports or train stations) may not use meters or may quote inflated prices to tourists.
   ◆ **Avoid it**: Use trusted apps like **Yandex Go** or **InDrive**, or agree on a price beforehand.

2. **Fake Police Officers** 👮: A rare but reported scam involves individuals posing as police and asking for passports or on-the-spot fines.
   ◆ **Avoid it**: Always ask for proper ID, and never hand over your passport without reason. Offer to go to the nearest station.

3. **Currency Exchange Tricks** 💱: Street money changers may use sleight of hand, shortchanging you or giving counterfeit notes.

◆ **Avoid it**: Exchange money only at **licensed exchange offices** or banks. Count your money in front of the teller.

4. **Restaurant Menu Swap** 🍽: Tourists have reported cases where menu prices change suddenly after ordering, or extra items are added to the bill.

   ◆ **Avoid it**: Always keep a photo of the menu or ask for a receipt. Avoid restaurants that don't clearly show prices.

5. **"Helpful" Strangers Offering Tours or Help** 🚶: Someone may offer to guide you or help with transport, only to demand payment later.

   ◆ **Avoid it**: Stick with **licensed guides** or those booked through official platforms.

6. **Pickpocketing in Crowded Areas** 👝: Especially during festivals, in bazaars, or on public transport.

   ◆ **Avoid it**: Keep your valuables close, preferably in a crossbody bag or money belt. Be alert in crowds.

What to Do in Case of Lost Passport or Illness

📄 If You Lose Your Passport:

1. **Report it to the Local Police**
   - File a police report immediately and get a copy or reference number.
   - Visit the nearest police station or call ☎ **102**.

2. **Contact Your Embassy**
   - They will help you get an emergency travel document or a replacement passport.
   - Bring ID copies, passport photos, and the police report.

🔑 **Pro Tip**: Always carry a photocopy of your passport and visa in a separate place from your original documents.

😷 If You Fall Ill or Have a Medical Emergency:

1. **Call Emergency Medical Services**
   - Dial ☎ **103** or **112** for ambulance and general emergencies.

2. **Visit an International Clinic (especially in Almaty or Astana)**

Recommended:

- o **International SOS Clinic (Almaty)**

  📍 91 Dostyk Ave

  ☎ +7 727 258 1911

  🌐 internationalsos.com

- o **Mediker Hospital (Astana)**

  📍 4 Imanbaeva St

  ☎ +7 7172 79 89 89

  🌐 mediker.kz

3. **Use Travel Insurance**

- o Present your insurance card to get coverage for treatments.
- o If you need to pay first, keep all receipts for reimbursement.

4. **Pharmacies (Аптека)**

- o Widely available in cities. Ask for English-speaking staff or use a translation app.
- o **Helpful App**: *Google Translate* with photo text recognition works well for medicine labels.

Departure Tips and Airport Navigation

Leaving Kazakhstan can be just as smooth as arriving — if you're prepared. Whether you're departing from **Nursultan Nazarbayev International Airport (NQZ)** in Astana or **Almaty International Airport (ALA)**, these tips will help you avoid last-minute stress and breeze through your final moments in the country.

🕐 1. Arrive Early

- **International Flights:** Arrive **3 hours** before departure.
- **Domestic Flights:** Arrive **1.5–2 hours** early. Security and customs can be time-consuming during busy travel seasons.

🧳 2. Check Your Baggage and Carry-on Limits

Each airline differs slightly, but general guidelines:

- **Checked Baggage:** 20–30 kg (economy), varies by carrier.
- **Carry-On:** Usually 1 piece (7–10 kg) + personal item.

- Avoid packing souvenirs like horse meat sausage (kazy) or fermented drinks in your hand luggage unless allowed.

3. Passport, Visa & Registration Check

- Ensure your **passport is valid** for at least 6 months beyond your departure.
- If you registered with local migration services (required for stays over 5 days in some cases), bring **registration slips** or documents.
- Some travelers may be asked to show their **migration card**, typically stamped at entry.

4. Spend or Exchange Leftover Tenge

- Use up Kazakhstani **Tenge (KZT)** at airport shops or restaurants.
- Alternatively, **exchange it at airport kiosks** before passing through security.
  Note: Airport exchange rates are often less favorable than city banks.

🔍 5. Know the Airport Layout

Both major airports offer:

- **Duty-Free Shops:** Local sweets, crafts, and Kazakh-branded items.
- **Food & Drink:** Cafés, fast food, and lounges.
- **Wi-Fi:** Free but may require phone number verification.
- **Prayer Rooms and Baby Rooms** available in international terminals.
- **Language:** Most signs are in Kazakh, Russian, and English.

🛂 6. Security and Customs

- Standard international rules apply: no liquids over 100ml in hand luggage, etc.
- **Declare** any antiques, artworks, or rare minerals purchased.
- Some herbal medicines or local remedies may be subject to restrictions.

🚕 7. Getting to the Airport

- **Almaty (ALA):** Around 25–30 minutes from city center (taxi or Yandex Go).
- **Astana (NQZ):** Around 20–30 minutes from downtown.
- Most hotels can **arrange a transfer**, or you can pre-book a taxi.

🌐 Bonus Tip: Mobile Boarding & Apps

- Most major airlines serving Kazakhstan support **mobile check-in and e-boarding passes**.
- Use the **official airport apps or airline apps** (e.g., Air Astana, SCAT) for real-time updates.

Conclusion

Your Kazakh Adventure Awaits — Now and Always

Kazakhstan is not just a destination—it's a journey into a world where time slows down to let your senses absorb the magnificence of untouched landscapes, timeless traditions, and deeply rooted hospitality. From the soaring peaks of the Tian Shan Mountains to the whispering sands of the Singing Dunes, from the ancient Silk Road towns to the ultramodern cityscapes of Astana and Almaty—Kazakhstan will leave a vivid, enduring imprint on your heart.

This travel guide has taken you through every corner of this extraordinary land, unveiling iconic sights and secret escapes, cultural rituals and modern delights, wild adventures and tranquil retreats. Whether you came in search of adrenaline or spiritual renewal, cultural enrichment or authentic connection—you'll leave with stories, friendships, and perspectives you never anticipated.

💬 **But the true beauty of Kazakhstan lies not just in what you see—it's in how it makes you feel.** It's the nomadic heartbeat you sense in the wind-blown steppes. It's the comforting embrace of a stranger offering tea and bread. It's the echo of eagle calls in the highlands, and the scent of fresh baursak in a village home. It's the realization that somewhere so far from your own world can feel unexpectedly like home.

🕑 Carry Kazakhstan With You

As you pack your souvenirs and tuck away your boarding pass, remember to carry something far more precious:

- **Respect for cultures unlike your own.**
- **Gratitude for every local handshake and heartfelt smile.**
- **And a spark of curiosity that doesn't fade with the last flight.**

Kazakhstan has opened its arms to you. Let this guide remain a trusted companion for your next visit—because **one trip is never enough.** There's always another yurt to sleep in, another canyon to hike, another story to hear from a local elder.

🛫 Until We Meet Again...

Whether you're a solo traveler navigating unmarked roads, a family discovering yurts and fairytales, a food lover tasting fermented mare's milk for the first time, or a digital nomad sipping coffee in a leafy Almaty café—you are now part of the tapestry that makes Kazakhstan so unique.

So keep your memories close, share your stories, inspire others to explore this lesser-known wonderland, and perhaps… plan your return.

Kazakhstan is calling. Will you answer again?

"Once you've breathed the wild air of the Kazakh steppe, a part of you will forever ride with the wind."

Safe travels, explorer. ✈ KZ

Printed in Dunstable, United Kingdom